A RECORD OF BUDDHISTIC KINGDOMS BEING AN ACCOUNT BY THE CHINESE MONK FA-HIEN OF HIS TRAVELS IN INDIA AND CEYLON (A.D. 399-414)

VI. THE DEVAS CELEBRATING THE ATTAINMENT OF THE BUDDHASHIP. Ch. 31.

A RECORD OF BUDDHISTIC KINGDOMS BEING AN ACCOUNT BY THE CHINESE MONK FA-HIEN OF HIS TRAVELS IN INDIA AND CEYLON (A.D. 399-414)

IN SEARCH OF THE BUDDHIST BOOKS OF DISCIPLINE

TRANSLATED AND ANNOTATED
WITH A KOREAN RECENSION OF THE CHINESE TEXT

JAMES LEGGE

GYAN

Published by

Gyan Publishing House
5, Ansari Road
Daryaganj, New Delhi-110002
Phone: 011-47034999, 9811692060
E-mail: books@gyanbooks.com

Distribution Network
gyanbooks.com
India, USA, Canada, UK, Australia, France

ISBN : 978-81-212-3943-1 (PB)
First Published, Oxford, 1886

2nd Impression 2020

Printed at: Gyan Press, Delhi.

A
Record of Buddhistic Kingdoms Being an Account By
The Chinese Monk Fa-hien of
His Travels in India and Ceylon
(A.D. 399-414)
Author: James Legge

CONTENTS.

PAGE

PREFACE xi

INTRODUCTION.

LIFE OF FÂ-HIEN; GENUINENESS AND INTEGRITY OF THE TEXT OF HIS NARRATIVE; NUMBER OF THE ADHERENTS OF BUDDHISM 1

CHAPTER I.

FROM CH'ANG-GAN TO THE SANDY DESERT 9

CHAPTER II.

ON TO SHEN-SHEN AND THENCE TO KHOTEN 12

CHAPTER III.

KHOTEN. PROCESSIONS OF IMAGES. THE KING'S NEW MONASTERY . . 16

CHAPTER IV.

THROUGH THE TS'UNG OR 'ONION' MOUNTAINS TO K'EEH-CH'Â; PROBABLY SKARDO, OR SOME CITY MORE TO THE EAST IN LADAK 21

CHAPTER V.

GREAT QUINQUENNIAL ASSEMBLY OF MONKS. RELICS OF BUDDHA. PRODUCTIONS OF THE COUNTRY 22

CHAPTER VI.

ON TOWARDS NORTH INDIA. DARADA. IMAGE OF MAITREYA BODHISATTVA . 24

CHAPTER VII.

CROSSING OF THE INDUS. WHEN BUDDHISM FIRST CROSSED THAT RIVER FOR THE EAST 26

PAGE

CHAPTER VIII.

Woo-chang, or Udyâna. Monasteries and their ways. Traces of Buddha 28

CHAPTER IX.

Soo-ho-to. Legend of Buddha 30

CHAPTER X.

Gandhâra. Legends of Buddha 31

CHAPTER XI.

Takshaśilâ. Legends. The four great topes 32

CHAPTER XII.

Purushapura, or Peshâwur. Prophecy about king Kanishka and his tope. Buddha's alms-bowl. Death of Hwuy-ying . . . 33

CHAPTER XIII.

Nagâra. Festival of Buddha's skull-bone. Other relics, and his shadow 36

CHAPTER XIV.

Death of Hwuy-king in the Little Snowy mountains. Lo-e. Pohnâ. Crossing the Indus to the East 40

CHAPTER XV.

Bhida. Sympathy of monks with the pilgrims 41

CHAPTER XVI.

On to Mathurâ, or Muttra. Condition and customs of Central India; of the monks, vihâras, and monasteries 42

CHAPTER XVII.

Sankâśya. Buddha's ascent to and descent from the Trayastriṃśas heaven, and other legends 47

CHAPTER XVIII.

Kanyâkubja, or Canouge. Buddha's preaching 53

CHAPTER XIX.

Shâ-che. Legend of Buddha's Danta-kâshṭha 54

PAGE

CHAPTER XX.

Kośala and Śrâvastî. The Jetavana vihâra and other memorials and legends of Buddha. Sympathy of the monks with the pilgrims . 55

CHAPTER XXI.

The three predecessors of Śâkyamuni in the Buddhaship . . . 63

CHAPTER XXII.

Kapilavastu. Its desolation. Legends of Buddha's birth, and other incidents in connexion with it 64

CHAPTER XXIII.

Râma, and its tope 68

CHAPTER XXIV.

Where Buddha finally renounced the world, and where he died . 70

CHAPTER XXV.

Vaiśâlî. The tope called 'Weapons laid down.' The Council of Vaiśâlî 72

CHAPTER XXVI.

Remarkable death of Ânanda 75

CHAPTER XXVII.

Pâṭaliputtra, or Patna, in Magadha. King Aśoka's spirit-built palace and halls. The Buddhist Brahman, Râdhasâmi. Dispensaries and hospitals 77

CHAPTER XXVIII.

Râjagṛiha, New and Old. Legends and incidents connected with it . 80

CHAPTER XXIX.

Gṛidhra-kûṭa hill, and legends. Fâ-hien passes a night on it. His reflections 82

CHAPTER XXX.

The Śrataparṇa cave, or cave of the First Council. Legends. Suicide of a Bhikshu 84

PAGE

CHAPTER XXXI.

GAYÂ. ŚÂKYAMUNI'S ATTAINING TO THE BUDDHASHIP; AND OTHER LEGENDS . 87

CHAPTER XXXII.

LEGEND OF KING AŚOKA IN A FORMER BIRTH, AND HIS NARAKA . . 90

CHAPTER XXXIII.

MOUNT GURUPADA, WHERE KAŚYAPA BUDDHA'S ENTIRE SKELETON IS . 92

CHAPTER XXXIV.

ON THE WAY BACK TO PATNA. VÂRÂṆASÎ, OR BENÂRES. ŚÂKYAMUNI'S FIRST DOINGS AFTER BECOMING BUDDHA 93

CHAPTER XXXV.

DAKSHIṆA, AND THE PIGEON MONASTERY 96

CHAPTER XXXVI.

IN PATNA. FÂ-HIEN'S LABOURS IN TRANSCRIPTION OF MANUSCRIPTS, AND INDIAN STUDIES FOR THREE YEARS 98

CHAPTER XXXVII.

TO CHAMPÂ AND TÂMALIPTÎ. STAY AND LABOURS THERE FOR THREE YEARS. TAKES SHIP TO SINGHALA, OR CEYLON 100

CHAPTER XXXVIII.

AT CEYLON. RISE OF THE KINGDOM. FEATS OF BUDDHA. TOPES AND MONASTERIES. STATUE OF BUDDHA IN JADE. BO TREE. FESTIVAL OF BUDDHA'S TOOTH 101

CHAPTER XXXIX.

CREMATION OF AN ARHAT. SERMON OF A DEVOTEE 107

CHAPTER XL.

AFTER TWO YEARS TAKES SHIP FOR CHINA. DISASTROUS PASSAGE TO JAVA; AND THENCE TO CHINA; ARRIVES AT SHAN-TUNG; AND GOES TO NANKING. CONCLUSION OR L'ENVOI BY ANOTHER WRITER . . . 111

LIST OF ILLUSTRATIONS, &c.

SKETCH MAP OF FÂ-HIEN'S TRAVELS . . . *To face Introduction, page* 1

I.

DREAM OF BUDDHA'S MOTHER OF HIS INCARNATION . . . *To face p.* 65

II.

BUDDHA JUST BORN, WITH THE NÂGAS SUPPLYING WATER TO WASH HIM . . . . *To face p.* 67

III.

BUDDHA TOSSING THE WHITE ELEPHANT OVER THE WALL . . *To face p.* 66

IV.

BUDDHA IN SOLITUDE AND ENDURING AUSTERITIES . . . *To face p.* 87

V.

BUDDHASHIP ATTAINED . . . . *To face p.* 88

VI.

THE DEVAS CELEBRATING THE ATTAINMENT OF THE BUDDHASHIP . *To face the Title*

VII.

BUDDHA'S DYING INSTRUCTIONS . . . . *To face p.* 70

VIII.

BUDDHA'S DEATH . . . . *To follow* VII

IX.

DIVISION OF BUDDHA'S RELICS . . . . *To follow* VIII

PREFACE.

SEVERAL times during my long residence in Hong Kong I endeavoured to read through the 'Narrative of Fâ-hien;' but though interested with the graphic details of much of the work, its columns bristled so constantly—now with his phonetic representations of Sanskrit words, and now with his substitution for them of their meanings in Chinese characters, and I was, moreover, so much occupied with my own special labours on the Confucian Classics, that my success was far from satisfactory. When Dr. Eitel's 'Handbook for the Student of Chinese Buddhism' appeared in 1870, the difficulty occasioned by the Sanskrit words and names was removed, but the other difficulty remained; and I was not able to look into the book again for several years. Nor had I much inducement to do so in the two copies of it which I had been able to procure, on poor paper, and printed from blocks badly cut at first, and so worn with use as to yield books the reverse of attractive in their appearance to the student.

In the meantime I kept studying the subject of Buddhism from various sources; and in 1878 began to lecture, here in Oxford, on the Travels with my Davis Chinese scholar, who was at the same time Boden Sanskrit scholar. As we went on, I wrote out a translation in English for my own satisfaction of nearly half the narrative. In the beginning of last year I made Fâ-hien again the subject of lecture, wrote out a second translation, independent of the former, and pushed on till I had completed the whole.

The want of a good and clear text had been supplied by my friend,

Mr. Bunyiu Nanjio, who sent to me from Japan a copy, the text of which is appended to the translation and notes, and of the nature of which some account is given in the Introduction (page 4), and towards the end of this Preface.

The present work consists of three parts: the Translation of Fâ-hien's Narrative of his Travels; copious Notes; and the Chinese Text of my copy from Japan.

It is for the Translation that I hold myself more especially responsible. Portions of it were written out three times, and the whole of it twice. While preparing my own version I made frequent reference to previous translations:—those of M. Abel Rémusat, 'Revu, complété, et augmenté d'éclaircissements nouveaux par MM. Klaproth et Landresse' (Paris, 1836); of the Rev. Samuel Beal (London, 1869), and his revision of it, prefixed to his 'Buddhist Records of the Western World' (Trübner's Oriental Series, 1884); and of Mr. Herbert A. Giles, of H. M.'s Consular Service in China (1877). To these I have to add a series of articles on 'Fa-hsien and his English Translators,' by Mr. T. Watters, British Consul at Î-Chang (China Review, 1879, 1880). Those articles are of the highest value, displaying accuracy of Chinese scholarship and an extensive knowledge of Buddhism. I have regretted that Mr. Watters, while reviewing others, did not himself write out and publish a version of the whole of Fâ-hien's narrative. If he had done so, I should probably have thought that, on the whole, nothing more remained to be done for the distinguished Chinese pilgrim in the way of translation. Mr. Watters had to judge of the comparative merits of the versions of Beal and Giles, and pronounce on the many points of contention between them. I have endeavoured to eschew those matters, and have seldom made remarks of a critical nature in defence of renderings of my own.

The Chinese narrative runs on without any break. It was Klaproth who divided Rémusat's translation into forty chapters. The division is helpful to the reader, and I have followed it excepting in three or four instances. In the reprinted Chinese text the chapters are separated by a circle (O) in the column.

In transliterating the names of Chinese characters I have generally followed the spelling of Morrison rather than the Pekinese, which is now in vogue. We cannot tell exactly what the pronunciation of them was, about fifteen hundred years ago, in the time of Fâ-hien; but the southern mandarin must be a shade nearer to it than that of Peking at the present day. In transliterating the Indian names I have for the most part followed Dr. Eitel, with such modification as seemed good and in harmony with growing usage.

For the Notes I can do little more than claim the merit of selection and condensation. My first object in them was to explain what in the text required explanation to an English reader. All Chinese texts, and Buddhist texts especially, are new to foreign students. One has to do for them what many hundreds of the ablest scholars in Europe have done for the Greek and Latin Classics during several hundred years, and what the thousands of critics and commentators have been doing for our Sacred Scriptures for nearly eighteen centuries. There are few predecessors in the field of Chinese literature into whose labours translators of the present century can enter. This will be received, I hope, as a sufficient apology for the minuteness and length of some of the notes. A second object in them was to teach myself first, and then others, something of the history and doctrines of Buddhism. I have thought that they might be learned better in connexion with a lively narrative like that of Fâ-hien than by reading didactic descriptions and argumentative books. Such has been my own experience. The books which I have consulted for these notes have been many, besides Chinese works. My principal help has been the full and masterly handbook of Eitel, mentioned already, and often referred to as E. H. Spence Hardy's 'Eastern Monachism' (E. M.) and 'Manual of Buddhism' (M. B.) have been constantly in hand, as well as Rhys Davids' Buddhism, published by the Society for Promoting Christian Knowledge, his Hibbert Lectures, and his Buddhist Suttas in the Sacred Books of the East, and other writings. I need not mention other authorities, having endeavoured always to specify them where I make use of them. My proximity and access to the Bodleian Library and the Indian Institute have been of great advantage.

I may be allowed to say that, so far as my own study of it has gone, I think there are many things in the vast field of Buddhistic literature which still require to be carefully handled. How far, for instance, are we entitled to regard the present Sûtras as genuine and sufficiently accurate copies of those which were accepted by the Councils before our Christian era? Can anything be done to trace the rise of the legends and marvels of Śâkyamuni's history, which were current so early (as it seems to us) as the time of Fâ-hien, and which startle us so frequently by similarities between them and narratives in our Gospels? Dr. Hermann Oldenberg, certainly a great authority on Buddhistic subjects, says that 'a biography of Buddha has not come down to us from ancient times, from the age of the Pâli texts; and, we can safely say, no such biography existed then' ('Buddha—His Life, His Doctrine, His Order,' as translated by Hoey, p. 78). He has also (in the same work, pp. 99, 416, 417) come to the conclusion that the hitherto unchallenged tradition that the Buddha was 'a king's son' must be given up. The name, 'king's son' (in Chinese 太子), always used of the Buddha, certainly requires to be understood in the highest sense. I am content myself to wait for further information on these and other points, as the result of prolonged and careful research.

Dr. Rhys Davids has kindly read the proofs of the Translation and Notes, and I most cordially thank him for doing so, for his many valuable corrections in the Notes, and for other suggestions which I have received from him. I may not always think on various points exactly as he does, but I am not more forward than he is to say with Horace,—

'Nullius addictus jurare in verba magistri.'

I have referred above, and also in the Introduction, to the Corean text of Fâ-hien's narrative, which I received from Mr. Nanjio. It is on the whole so much superior to the better-known texts, that I determined to attempt to reproduce it at the end of the little volume, so far as our resources here in Oxford would permit. To do so has not been an easy task. The two fonts of Chinese types in the Clarendon Press were prepared primarily for printing the translation of our Sacred

Scriptures, and then extended so as to be available for printing also the Confucian Classics; but a Buddhist work necessarily requires many types not found in them, while many other characters in the Corean recension are peculiar in their forms, and some are what Chinese dictionaries denominate 'vulgar.' That we have succeeded so well as we have done is owing chiefly to the intelligence, ingenuity, and untiring attention of Mr. J. C. Pembrey, the Oriental Reader.

The pictures that have been introduced were taken from a superb edition of a History of Buddha, republished recently at Hang-châu in Cheh-kiang, and profusely illustrated in the best style of Chinese art. I am indebted for the use of it to the Rev. J. H. Sedgwick, University Chinese Scholar.

JAMES LEGGE.

OXFORD:
June, 1886.

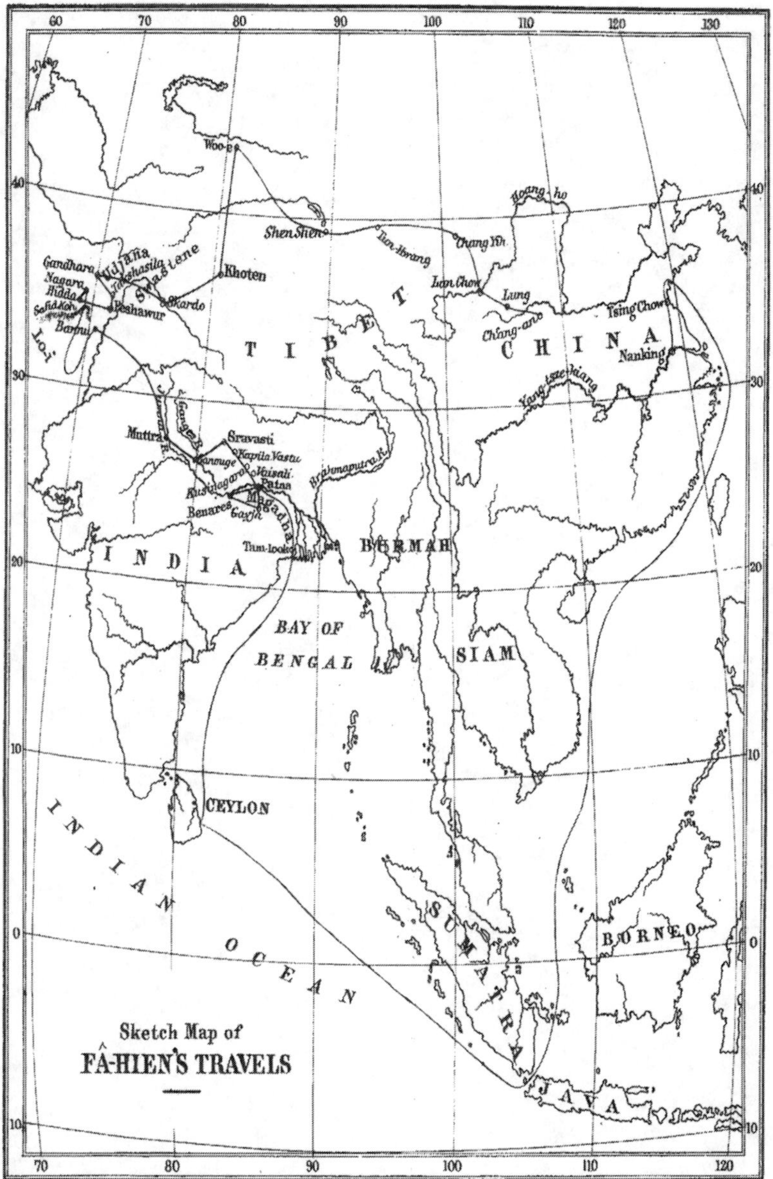

Sketch Map of
FÂ-HIEN'S TRAVELS

University Press, Oxford.

INTRODUCTION.

LIFE OF FÂ-HIEN; GENUINENESS AND INTEGRITY OF THE TEXT OF HIS NARRATIVE; NUMBER OF THE ADHERENTS OF BUDDHISM.

1. Nothing of great importance is known about Fâ-hien in addition to what may be gathered from his own record of his travels. I have read the accounts of him in the 'Memoirs of Eminent Monks,' compiled in A.D. 519, and a later work, the 'Memoirs of Marvellous Monks,' by the third emperor of the Ming dynasty (A.D. 1403–1424), which, however, is nearly all borrowed from the other; and all in them that has an appearance of verisimilitude can be brought within brief compass.

His surname, they tell us, was Kung[1], and he was a native of Wû-yang[2] in P'ing-yang[2], which is still the name of a large department in Shan-hsî. He had three brothers older than himself; but when they all died before shedding their first teeth, his father devoted him to the service of the Buddhist society, and had him entered as a Śrâmaṇera, still keeping him at home in the family. The little fellow fell dangerously ill, and the father sent him to the monastery, where he soon got well and refused to return to his parents.

When he was ten years old, his father died; and an uncle, considering the widowed solitariness and helplessness of the mother, urged him to renounce the monastic life, and return to her, but the boy replied, 'I did not quit the family in compliance with my father's wishes, but because I wished to be far from the dust and vulgar ways of life. This is why I choose monkhood.' The uncle approved of his words and gave over

---

[1] 龔.

[2] 平陽, 武陽.

urging him. When his mother also died, it appeared how great had been the affection for her of his fine nature; but after her burial he returned to the monastery.

On one occasion he was cutting rice with a score or two of his fellow-disciples, when some hungry thieves came upon them to take away their grain by force. The other Śrâmaṇeras all fled, but our young hero stood his ground, and said to the thieves, 'If you must have the grain, take what you please. But, Sirs, it was your former neglect of charity which brought you to your present state of destitution; and now, again, you wish to rob others. I am afraid that in the coming ages you will have still greater poverty and distress;—I am sorry for you beforehand.' With these words he followed his companions to the monastery, while the thieves left the grain and went away, all the monks, of whom there were several hundred, doing homage to his conduct and courage.

When he had finished his noviciate and taken on him the obligations of the full Buddhist orders, his earnest courage, clear intelligence, and strict regulation of his demeanour were conspicuous; and soon after, he undertook his journey to India in search of complete copies of the Vinaya-piṭaka. What follows this is merely an account of his travels in India and return to China by sea, condensed from his own narrative, with the addition of some marvellous incidents that happened to him, on his visit to the Vulture Peak near Râjagṛiha.

It is said in the end that after his return to China, he went to the capital (evidently Nanking), and there, along with the Indian Śramaṇa Buddha-bhadra, executed translations of some of the works which he had obtained in India; and that before he had done all that he wished to do in this way, he removed to King-chow[1] (in the present Hoo-pih), and died in the monastery of Sin, at the age of eighty-eight, to the great sorrow of all who knew him. It is added that there is another larger work giving an account of his travels in various countries.

Such is all the information given about our author, beyond what he

---

[1] 荆州.

has himself told us. Fâ-hien was his clerical name, and means 'Illustrious in the Law,' or 'Illustrious master of the Law.' The Shih which often precedes it is an abbreviation of the name of Buddha as Śâkyamuni, 'the Śâkya, mighty in Love, dwelling in Seclusion and Silence,' and may be taken as equivalent to Buddhist. He is sometimes said to have belonged to 'the eastern Tsin dynasty' (A.D. 317–419), and sometimes to 'the Sung,' that is, the Sung dynasty of the House of Liû (A.D. 420–478). If he became a full monk at the age of twenty, and went to India when he was twenty-five, his long life may have been divided pretty equally between the two dynasties.

2. If there were ever another and larger account of Fâ-hien's travels than the narrative of which a translation is now given, it has long ceased to be in existence.

In the Catalogue of the imperial library of the Suy dynasty (A.D. 589–618), the name Fâ-hien occurs four times. Towards the end of the last section of it (page 22), after a reference to his travels, his labours in translation at Kin-ling (another name for Nanking), in conjunction with Buddha-bhadra, are described. In the second section, page 15, we find 'A Record of Buddhistic Kingdoms;'—with a note, saying that it was the work of 'the Śramaṇa, Fâ-hien;' and again, on page 13, we have 'Narrative of Fâ-hien in two Books,' and 'Narrative of Fâ-hien's Travels in one Book.' But all these three entries may possibly belong to different copies of the same work, the first and the other two being in separate subdivisions of the Catalogue.

In the two Chinese copies of the narrative in my possession the title is 'Record of Buddhistic Kingdoms.' In the Japanese or Corean recension subjoined to this translation, the title is twofold; first, 'Narrative of the Distinguished Monk, Fâ-hien;' and then, more at large, 'Incidents of Travels in India, by the Śramaṇa of the Eastern Tsin, Fâ-hien, recorded by himself.'

There is still earlier attestation of the existence of our little work than the Suy Catalogue. The Catalogue Raisonné of the imperial library of the present dynasty (chap. 71) mentions two quotations from it by Le Tâo-yüen, a geographical writer of the dynasty of the Northern Wei

(A.D. 386–584), one of them containing 89 characters, and the other 276; both of them given as from the 'Narrative of Fâ-hien.'

In all catalogues subsequent to that of Suy our work appears. The evidence for its authenticity and genuineness is all that could be required. It is clear to myself that the 'Record of Buddhistic Kingdoms' and the 'Narrative of his Travels by Fâ-hien' were designations of one and the same work, and that it is doubtful whether any larger work on the same subject was ever current. With regard to the text subjoined to my translation, it was published in Japan in 1779. The editor had before him four recensions of the narrative; those of the Sung and Ming dynasties, with appendixes on the names of certain characters in them; that of Japan; and that of Corea. He wisely adopted the Corean text, published in accordance with a royal rescript in 1726, so far as I can make out; but the different readings of the other texts are all given in top-notes, instead of foot-notes as with us, this being one of the points in which customs in the east and west go by contraries. Very occasionally, the editor indicates by a single character, equivalent to 'right' or 'wrong,' which reading in his opinion is to be preferred. In the notes to the present republication of the Corean text, S stands for Sung, M for Ming, and J for Japanese; R for right, and W for wrong. I have taken the trouble to give all the various readings (amounting to more than 300), partly as a curiosity and to make my text complete, and partly to show how, in the transcription of writings in whatever language, such variations are sure to occur,

> ' maculae, quas aut incuria fudit,
> Aut humana parum cavit natura,'

while on the whole they very slightly affect the meaning of the document.

The editors of the Catalogue Raisonné intimate their doubts of the good taste and reliability of all Fâ-hien's statements. It offends them that he should call central India the 'Middle Kingdom,' and China, which to them was the true and only Middle Kingdom, but 'a Border land;'—it offends them as the vaunting language of a Buddhist writer, whereas the reader will see in the expressions only an instance of what Fâ-hien calls his 'simple straightforwardness.'

As an instance of his unreliability they refer to his account of the Buddhism of Khoten, whereas it is well known, they say, that the Khoteners from ancient times till now have been Mohammedans;—as if they could have been so 170 years before Mohammed was born, and 222 years before the year of the Hegira! And this is criticism in China. The Catalogue was ordered by the K'ien-lung emperor in 1722. Between three and four hundred of the 'Great Scholars' of the empire were engaged on it in various departments, and thus egregiously ignorant did they show themselves of all beyond the limits of their own country, and even of the literature of that country itself.

Much of what Fâ-hien tells his readers of Buddhist miracles and legends is indeed unreliable and grotesque; but we have from him the truth as to what he saw and heard.

3. In concluding this introduction I wish to call attention to some estimates of the number of Buddhists in the world which have become current, believing, as I do, that the smallest of them is much above what is correct.

i. In a note on the first page of his work on the Bhilsa Topes (1854), General Cunningham says: 'The Christians number about 270 millions; the Buddhists about 222 millions, who are distributed as follows:—China 170 millions, Japan 25, Anam 14, Siam 3, Ava 8, Nepál 1, and Ceylon 1; total, 222 millions.'

ii. In his article on M. J. Barthélemy Saint Hilaire's 'Le Bouddha et sa Religion,' republished in his 'Chips from a German Workshop,' vol. i. (1868), Professor Max Müller (p. 215) says, 'The young prince became the founder of a religion which, after more than two thousand years, is still professed by 455 millions of human beings,' and he appends the following note: 'Though truth is not settled by majorities, it would be interesting to know which religion counts at the present moment the largest numbers of believers. Berghaus, in his "Physical Atlas," gives the following division of the human race according to religion:—"Buddhists 31.2 per cent, Christians 30.7, Mohammedans 15.7, Brahmanists 13.4, Heathens 8.7, and Jews 0.3." As Berghaus does not distinguish the Buddhists in China from the followers of Confucius and Laotse, the first place on the scale belongs really to Christianity. It is difficult in China to say to what religion a man belongs, as the same person may profess two or three. The emperor himself, after sacrificing according to the ritual of Confucius, visits a Tao-ssé temple, and afterwards bows before an image of Fo in a Buddhist chapel. ("Mélanges Asiatiques de St. Pétersbourg," vol. ii. p. 374.)'

iii. Both these estimates are exceeded by Dr. T. W. Rhys Davids (intimating also the uncertainty of the statements, and that numbers are no evidence of truth) in the introduction to his 'Manual of Buddhism.' The Buddhists there appear as amounting in all to 500 millions:—30 millions of Southern Buddhists, in Ceylon, Burma, Siam, Anam, and India (Jains); and 470 millions of Northern Buddhists, of whom nearly 33 millions are assigned to Japan, and 414,686,974 to the eighteen provinces of China proper. According to him, Christians amount to about 26 per cent of mankind, Hindus to about 13, Mohammedans to about 12½, Buddhists to about 40, and Jews to about ½.

In regard to all these estimates, it will be observed that the immense numbers assigned to Buddhism are made out by the multitude of Chinese with which it is credited. Subtract Cunningham's 170 millions of Chinese from his total of 222, and there remains only 52 millions of Buddhists. Subtract Davids' (say) 414½ millions of Chinese from his total of 500, and there remain only 85½ millions for Buddhism. Of the numbers assigned to other countries, as well as of their whole populations, I am in considerable doubt, excepting in the cases of Ceylon and India; but the greatness of the estimates turns upon the immense multitudes said to be in China. I do not know what total population Cunningham allowed for that country, nor on what principle he allotted 170 millions of it to Buddhism;—perhaps he halved his estimate of the whole, whereas Berghaus and Davids allotted to it the highest estimates that have been given of the people.

But we have no certain information of the population of China. At an interview with the former Chinese ambassador, Kwo Sung-tâo, in Paris, in 1878, I begged him to write out for me the amount, with the authority for it, and he assured me that it could not be done. I have read probably almost everything that has been published on the subject, and endeavoured by methods of my own to arrive at a satisfactory conclusion;—without reaching a result which I can venture to lay before the public. My impression has been that 400 millions is hardly an exaggeration.

But supposing that we had reliable returns of the whole population, how shall we proceed to apportion that among Confucianists, Tâoists, and Buddhists? Confucianism is the orthodoxy of China. The common name for it is Jû Chiâo, 'the Doctrines held by the Learned Class,' entrance into the circle of which is, with a few insignificant exceptions, open to all the people. The mass of them and the masses under their influence are preponderatingly Confucian; and in the observance of ancestral worship, the most remarkable feature of the religion proper of China from the earliest times, of which Confucius was not the author but the prophet, an overwhelming majority are regular and assiduous.

Among 'the strange principles' which the emperor of the K'ang-hsî period, in one of his famous Sixteen Precepts, exhorted his people to 'discountenance and put away, in order to exalt the correct doctrine,' Buddhism and Tâoism were both included. If, as stated in the note quoted from Professor Müller, the emperor countenances both the Tâoist worship and the Buddhist, he does so for reasons of state;—to please especially his Buddhistic subjects in Thibet and Mongolia, and not to offend the many whose superstitious fancies incline to Tâoism.

When I went out and in as a missionary among the Chinese people for about thirty years, it sometimes occurred to me that only the inmates of their monasteries and the recluses of both systems should be enumerated as Buddhists and Tâoists; but I was in the end constrained to widen that judgment, and to admit a considerable following of both among the people, who have neither received the tonsure nor assumed the yellow top. Dr. Eitel, in concluding his discussion of this point in his 'Lecture on Buddhism, an Event in History,' says: 'It is not too much to say that most Chinese are theoretically Confucianists, but emotionally Buddhists or Tâoists. But fairness requires us to add that, though the mass of the people are more or less influenced by Buddhist doctrines, yet the people, as a whole, have no respect for the Buddhist church, and habitually sneer at Buddhist priests.' For the 'most' in the former of these two sentences I would substitute 'nearly all;' and between my friend's 'but' and 'emotionally' I would introduce 'many are,' and would not care to contest his conclusion farther. It does seem to me preposterous to credit Buddhism with the whole of the vast population of China, the great majority of whom are Confucianists. My own opinion is, that its adherents are not so many as those even of Mohammedanism, and that instead of being the most numerous of the religions (so called) of the world, it is only entitled to occupy the fifth place, ranking below Christianity, Confucianism, Brahmanism, and Mohammedanism, and followed, some distance off, by Tâoism. To make a table of per-centages of mankind, and assign to each system its proportion, is to seem to be wise where we are deplorably ignorant; and, moreover, if our means of information were much better than they are, our figures would merely show the outward adherence. A fractional per-centage might tell more for one system than a very large integral one for another.

THE TRAVELS OF FÂ-HIEN,

OR

RECORD OF BUDDHISTIC KINGDOMS.

CHAPTER I.

FROM CH'ANG-GAN TO THE SANDY DESERT.

FÂ-HIEN had been living in Ch'ang-gan[1]. Deploring the mutilated and imperfect state of the collection of the Books of Discipline, in the second year of the period Hwăng-che, being the Ke-hâe year of the cycle[2], he entered into an engagement with Hwuy-king, Tâo-ching,

---

[1] Ch'ang-gan is still the name of the principal district (and its city) in the department of Se-gan, Shen-se. It had been the capital of the first empire of Han (B.C. 202–A.D. 24), as it subsequently was that of Suy (A.D. 589–618). The empire of the eastern Tsin, towards the close of which Fâ-hien lived, had its capital at or near Nan-king, and Ch'ang-gan was the capital of the principal of the three Ts'in kingdoms, which, with many other minor ones, maintained a semi-independence of Tsin, their rulers sometimes even assuming the title of emperor.

[2] The period Hwăng-che embraced from A.D. 399 to 414, being the greater portion of the reign of Yâo Hing of the After Ts'in, a powerful prince. He adopted Hwăng-che for the style of his reign in 399, and the cyclical name of that year was Kăng-tsze. It is not possible at this distance of time to explain, if it could be explained, how Fâ-hien came to say that Ke-hâe was the second year of the period. It seems most reasonable to suppose that he set out on his pilgrimage in A. D. 399, the cycle name of which was Ke-hâe, as 二, the second year, instead of 一, the first, might easily creep into the text. In the 'Memoirs of Eminent Monks' it is said that our author started in the third year of the period Lung-gan of the eastern Tsin, which was A. D. 399.

Hwuy-ying, and Hwuy-wei[1], that they should go to India and seek for the Disciplinary Rules[2].

After starting from Ch'ang-gan, they passed through Lung[3], and came to the kingdom of K'een-kwei[4], where they stopped for the summer retreat[5]. When that was over, they went forward to the kingdom of Now-t'an[6], crossed the mountain of Yang-low, and reached

---

[1] These, like Fâ-hien itself, are all what we might call 'clerical' names, appellations given to the parties as monks or śramaṇas.

[2] The Buddhist tripiṭaka or canon consists of three collections, containing, according to Eitel (p. 150), 'doctrinal aphorisms (or statements, purporting to be from Buddha himself); works on discipline; and works on metaphysics:'—called sûtra, vinaya, and abhidharma; in Chinese, king (經), leŭh (律), and lun (論), or texts, laws or rules, and discussions. Dr. Rhys Davids objects to the designation of 'metaphysics' as used of the abhidharma works, saying that 'they bear much more the relation to "dharma" which "by-law" bears to "law" than that which "metaphysics" bears to "physics"' (Hibbert Lectures, p. 49). However this be, it was about the vinaya works that Fâ-hien was chiefly concerned. He wanted a good code of the rules for the government of 'the Order' in all its internal and external relations.

[3] Lung embraced the western part of Shen-se and the eastern part of Kan-sŭh. The name remains in Lung Chow, in the extreme west of Shen-se.

[4] K'een-kwei was the second king of 'the Western Ts'in.' His family was of northern or barbarous origin, from the tribe of the Seen-pe, with the surname of K'eih-fuh. The first king was Kwo-jin, and received his appointment from the sovereign of the chief Ts'in kingdom in 385. He was succeeded in 388 by his brother, the K'een-kwei of the text, who was very prosperous in 398, and took the title of king of Ts'in. Fâ-hien would find him at his capital, somewhere in the present department of Lan-chow, Kan-sŭh.

[5] Under varshâs or varshâvasâna (Pâli, vassa; Spence Hardy, vass), Eitel (p. 163) says:—'One of the most ancient institutions of Buddhist discipline, requiring all ecclesiastics to spend the rainy season in a monastery in devotional exercises. Chinese Buddhists naturally substituted the hot season for the rainy (from the 16th day of the 5th to the 15th day of the 9th Chinese month).'

[6] During the troubled period of the Tsin dynasty, there were five (usurping) Leang sovereignties in the western part of the empire (五 凉). The name Leang remains in the department of Leang-chow in the northern part of Kan-sŭh. The 'southern Leang' arose in 397 under a T'ŭh-fâh Wû-kû, who was succeeded

the emporium of Chang-yih[1]. There they found the country so much disturbed that travelling on the roads was impossible for them. Its king, however, was very attentive to them, kept them (in his capital), and acted the part of their dânapati[2].

Here they met with Che-yen, Hwuy-keen, Săng-shâo, Pâo-yun, and Săng-king[3]; and in pleasant association with them, as bound on the same journey with themselves, they passed the summer retreat (of that year)[4] together, resuming after it their travelling, and going on to T'un-hwang[5], (the chief town) in the frontier territory of defence extending for about 80 le from east to west, and about 40 from north to south. Their company, increased as it had been, halted there for some days more than a month, after which Fâ-hien and his four friends started first in the suite of an envoy[6], having separated (for a time) from Pâo-yun and his associates.

---

in 399 by a brother, Le-luh-koo; and he again by his brother, the Now-t'an of the text, in 402, who was not yet king therefore when Fâ-hien and his friends reached his capital. How he is represented as being so may be accounted for in various ways, of which it is not necessary to write.

[1] Chang-yih is still the name of a district in Kan-chow department, Kan-sŭh. It is a long way north and west from Lan-chow, and not far from the Great Wall. Its king at this time was, probably, Twan-yeh of 'the northern Leang.'

[2] Dâna is the name for religious charity, the first of the six pâramitâs, or means of attaining to nirvâṇa; and a dânapati is 'one who practises dâna and thereby crosses (越) the sea of misery.' It is given as 'a title of honour to all who support the cause of Buddhism by acts of charity, especially to founders and patrons of monasteries;'—see Eitel, p. 29.

[3] Of these pilgrims with their clerical names, the most distinguished was Pâo-yun, who translated various Sanskrit works on his return from India, of which only one seems to be now existing. He died in 449. See Nanjio's Catalogue of the Tripiṭaka, col. 417.

[4] This was the second summer since the pilgrims left Ch'ang-gan. We are now therefore, probably, in A. D. 400.

[5] T'un-hwang (lat. 39° 40′ N.; lon. 94° 50′ E.) is still the name of one of the two districts constituting the department of Gan-se, the most western of the prefectures of Kan-sŭh; beyond the termination of the Great Wall.

[6] Who this envoy was, and where he was going, we do not know. The text will not admit of any other translation.

Le Hâo[1], the prefect of T'un-hwang, had supplied them with the means of crossing the desert (before them), in which there are many evil demons and hot winds. (Travellers) who encounter them perish all to a man. There is not a bird to be seen in the air above, nor an animal on the ground below. Though you look all round most earnestly to find where you can cross, you know not where to make your choice, the only mark and indication being the dry bones of the dead (left upon the sand)[2].

CHAPTER II.

ON TO SHEN-SHEN AND THENCE TO KHOTEN.

AFTER travelling for seventeen days, a distance we may calculate of about 1500 le, (the pilgrims) reached the kingdom of Shen-shen[3], a

---

[1] Le Hâo was a native of Lung-se, a man of learning, able and kindly in his government. He was appointed governor or prefect of T'un-hwang by the king of 'the northern Leang,' in 400; and there he sustained himself, becoming by and by 'duke of western Leang,' till he died in 417.

[2] 'The river of sand;' the great desert of Kobi or Gobi; having various other names. It was a great task which the pilgrims had now before them,—to cross this desert. The name of 'river' in the Chinese misleads the reader, and he thinks of the crossing it as of crossing a stream; but they had to traverse it from east to west. In his 'Vocabulary of Proper Names,' p. 23, Dr. Porter Smith says:—'It extends from the eastern frontier of Mongolia, south-westward to the further frontier of Turkestan, to within six miles of Ilchî, the chief town of Khoten. It thus comprises some twenty-three degrees of longitude in length, and from three to ten degrees of latitude in breadth, being about 2,100 miles in its greatest length. In some places it is arable. Some idea may be formed of the terror with which this "Sea of Sand," with its vast billows of shifting sands, is regarded, from the legend that in one of the storms 360 cities were all buried within the space of twenty-four hours.' See also Gilmour's 'Among the Mongols,' chap. 5.

[3] An account is given of the kingdom of Shen-shen in the 96th of the Books of the first Han dynasty, down to its becoming a dependency of China, about B.C. 80. The greater portion of that is now accessible to the English reader in a translation by Mr. Wylie in the 'Journal of the Anthropological Institute,' August, 1880. Mr. Wylie says:—'Although we may not

country rugged and hilly, with a thin and barren soil. The clothes of the common people are coarse, and like those worn in our land of Han [1], some wearing felt and others coarse serge or cloth of hair;—this was the only difference seen among them. The king professed (our) Law, and there might be in the country more than four thousand monks [2],

---

be able to identify Shen-shen with certainty, yet we have sufficient indications to give an approximate idea of its position, as being south of and not far from lake Lob.' He then goes into an exhibition of those indications, which I need not transcribe. It is sufficient for us to know that the capital city was not far from Lob or Lop Nor, into which in lon. 38° E. the Tarim flows. Fâ-hien estimated its distance to be 1500 le from T'un-hwang. He and his companions must have gone more than twenty-five miles a day to accomplish the journey in seventeen days.

[1] This is the name which Fâ-hien always uses when he would speak of China, his native country, as a whole, calling it from the great dynasty which had ruled it, first and last, for between four and five centuries. Occasionally, as we shall immediately see, he speaks of 'the territory of Ts'in or Ch'in,' but intending thereby only the kingdom of Ts'in, having its capital, as described in the first note on the last chapter, in Ch'ang-gan.

[2] So I prefer to translate the character 僧 (săng) rather than by 'priests.' Even in Christianity, beyond the priestly privilege which belongs to all believers, I object to the ministers of any denomination or church calling themselves or being called 'priests;' and much more is the name inapplicable to the śramaṇas or bhikshus of Buddhism which acknowledges no God in the universe, no soul in man, and has no services of sacrifice or prayer in its worship. The only difficulty in the use of 'monks' is caused by the members of the sect in Japan which, since the middle of the fifteenth century, has abolished the prohibition against marrying on the part of its ministers, and other prohibitions in diet and dress. Săng and săng-keâ represent the Sanskrit saṅgha, which denotes (E. H., p. 117), first, an assembly of monks, or bhikshu saṅgha, constituted by at least four members, and empowered to hear confession, to grant absolution, to admit persons to holy orders, &c.; secondly, the third constituent of the Buddhistic Trinity, a deification of the communio sanctorum, or the Buddhist order. The name is used by our author of the monks collectively or individually as belonging to the class, and may be considered as synonymous with the name śramaṇa, which will immediately claim our attention.

who were all students of the hînayâna[1]. The common people of this and other kingdoms (in that region), as well as the śramans[2], all practise the rules of India[3], only that the latter do so more exactly, and the former more loosely. So (the travellers) found it in all the kingdoms through which they went on their way from this to the west, only that each had its own peculiar barbarous speech[4]. (The monks), however, who had (given up the worldly life) and quitted their families, were all students of Indian books and the Indian language. Here they stayed for about a month, and then proceeded on their journey, fifteen days walking to the north-west bringing them to the country of Woo-e[5]. In this also there were more

---

[1] Meaning the 'small vehicle, or conveyance.' There are in Buddhism the triyâna, or 'three different means of salvation, i.e. of conveyance across the saṃsâra, or sea of transmigration, to the shores of nirvâṇa. Afterwards the term was used to designate the different phases of development through which the Buddhist dogma passed, known as the mahâyâna, hînayâna, and madhyamayâna.' 'The hînayâna is the simplest vehicle of salvation, corresponding to the first of the three degrees of saintship. Characteristics of it are the preponderance of active moral asceticism, and the absence of speculative mysticism and quietism.' E. H., pp. 151–2, 45, and 117.

[2] The name for India is here the same as in the former chapter and throughout the book,—T'een-chuh (天竺), the chuh being pronounced, probably, in Fâ-hien's time as tuk. How the earliest name for India, Shin-tuk or duk=Scinde, came to be changed into Thien-tuk, it would take too much space to explain. I believe it was done by the Buddhists, wishing to give a good auspicious name to the fatherland of their Law, and calling it 'the Heavenly Tuk,' just as the Mohammedans call Arabia 'the Heavenly region' (天方), and the court of China itself is called 'the Celestial' (天朝).

[3] 'Śraman' may in English take the place of Śramaṇa (Pâli, Samana; in Chinese, Shâ-măn), the name for Buddhist monks, as those who have separated themselves from (left) their families, and quieted their hearts from all intrusion of desire and lust. 'It is employed, first, as a general name for ascetics of all denominations, and, secondly, as a general designation of Buddhistic monks.' E. H., pp. 130, 131.

[4] Tartar or Mongolian.

[5] Woo-e has not been identified. Watters ('China Review,' viii. 115) says:— 'We cannot be far wrong if we place it in Kharaschar, or between that and

than four thousand monks, all students of the hînayâna. They were very strict in their rules, so that śramans from the territory of Ts'in[1] were all unprepared for their regulations. Fâ-hien, through the management of Foo Kung-sun, maître d'hôtellerie[2], was able to remain (with his company in the monastery where they were received) for more than two months, and here they were rejoined by Pâo-yun and his friends[3]. (At the end of that time) the people of Woo-e neglected the duties of propriety and righteousness, and treated the strangers in so niggardly a manner that Che-yen, Hwuy-keen, and Hwuy-wei went back towards Kâo-ch'ang[4], hoping to obtain there the means of continuing their journey. Fâ-hien and the rest, however, through the liberality of Foo Kung-sun, managed to go straight forward in a south-west direction. They found the country uninhabited as they went along. The difficulties

---

Kutscha.' It must have been a country of considerable size to have so many monks in it.

[1] This means in one sense China, but Fâ-hien, in his use of the name, was only thinking of the three Ts'in states of which I have spoken in a previous note; perhaps only of that from the capital of which he had himself set out.

[2] This sentence altogether is difficult to construe, and Mr. Watters, in the 'China Review,' was the first to disentangle more than one knot in it. I am obliged to adopt the reading of 行堂 in the Chinese editions, instead of the 行當 in the Corean text. It seems clear that only one person is spoken of as assisting the travellers, and his name, as appears a few sentences farther on, was Foo Kung-sun. The 行堂, which immediately follows the surname Foo (符), must be taken as the name of his office, corresponding, as the 行 shows, to that of le maître d'hôtellerie in a Roman Catholic abbey. I was once indebted myself to the kind help of such an officer at a monastery in Canton province. The Buddhistic name for him is uddesika,=overseer. The Kung-sun that follows his surname indicates that he was descended from some feudal lord in the old times of the Chow dynasty. We know indeed of no ruling house which had the surname of Foo, but its adoption by the grandson of a ruler can be satisfactorily accounted for; and his posterity continued to call themselves Kung-sun, duke or lord's grandson, and so retain the memory of the rank of their ancestor.

[3] Whom they had left behind them at T'un-hwang.

[4] The country of the Ouighurs, the district around the modern Turfan or Tangut.

which they encountered in crossing the streams and on their route, and the sufferings which they endured, were unparalleled in human experience, but in the course of a month and five days they succeeded in reaching Yu-teen [1].

CHAPTER III.

KHOTEN. PROCESSIONS OF IMAGES. THE KING'S NEW MONASTERY.

YU-TEEN is a pleasant and prosperous kingdom, with a numerous and flourishing population. The inhabitants all profess our Law, and join together in its religious music for their enjoyment [2]. The monks amount to several myriads, most of whom are students of the mahâyâna [3]. They all receive their food from the common store [4]. Throughout the

---

[1] Yu-teen is better known as Khoten. Dr. P. Smith gives (p. 11) the following description of it:—'A large district on the south-west of the desert of Gobi, embracing all the country south of Oksu and Yarkand, along the northern base of the Kwun-lun mountains, for more than 300 miles from east to west. The town of the same name, now called Ilchî, is in an extensive plain on the Khoten river, in lat. 37° N., and lon. 80° 35′ E. After the Tungâni insurrection against Chinese rule in 1862, the Mufti Hâji Habeeboolla was made governor of Khoten, and held the office till he was murdered by Yakoob Beg, who became for a time the conqueror of all Chinese Turkestan. Khoten produces fine linen and cotton stuffs, jade ornaments, copper, grain, and fruits.' The name in Sanskrit is Kustana (E. H., p. 60).

[2] This fondness for music among the Khoteners is mentioned by Hsüan Ch'wang and others.

[3] Mahâyâna; see note 1 on p. 14. It is a later form of the Buddhist doctrine, the second phase of its development corresponding to the state of a Bodhisattva, who, being able to transport himself and all mankind to nirvâṇa, may be compared to a huge vehicle. See Davids on the 'Key-note of the "Great Vehicle,"' Hibbert Lectures, p. 254.

[4] Fâ-hien supplies sufficient information of how the common store or funds of the monasteries were provided, farther on in chapters xvi and xxxix, as well as in other passages. As the point is important, I will give here, from Davids' fifth Hibbert Lecture (p. 178), some of the words of the dying Buddha, taken from 'The Book of the Great Decease,' as illustrating the statement in this text:—'So

country the houses of the people stand apart like (separate) stars, and each family has a small tope[1] reared in front of its door. The smallest of these may be twenty cubits high, or rather more[2]. They make (in the monasteries) rooms for monks from all quarters[2], the use of which is given to travelling monks who may arrive, and who are provided with whatever else they require.

The lord of the country lodged Fâ-hien and the others comfortably, and supplied their wants, in a monastery[3] called Gomati[3], of the mahâyâna school. Attached to it there are three thousand monks, who

---

long as the brethren shall persevere in kindness of action, speech, and thought among the saints, both in public and private; so long as they shall divide without partiality, and share in common with the upright and holy, all such things as they receive in accordance with the just provisions of the order, down even to the mere contents of a begging bowl; .... so long may the brethren be expected not to decline, but to prosper.'

[1] The Chinese 塔 (t'ah; in Cantonese, t'ap), as used by Fâ-hien, is, no doubt, a phonetisation of the Sanskrit stûpa or Pâli thûpa; and it is well in translating to use for the structures described by him the name of topes,—made familiar by Cunningham and other Indian antiquarians. In the thirteenth chapter there is an account of one built under the superintendence of Buddha himself, 'as a model for all topes in future.' They were usually in the form of bell-shaped domes, and were solid, surmounted by a long tapering pinnacle formed with a series of rings, varying in number. But their form, I suppose, was often varied; just as we have in China pagodas of different shapes. There are several topes now in the Indian Institute at Oxford, brought from Buddha Gâyâ, but the largest of them is much smaller than 'the smallest' of those of Khoten. They were intended chiefly to contain relics of Buddha and famous masters of his Law; but what relics could there be in the Triratna topes of chapter xvi?

[2] The meaning here is much disputed. The author does not mean to say that the monk's apartments were made 'square,' but that the monasteries were made with many guest-chambers or spare rooms.

[3] The Sanskrit term for a monastery is used here,—Saṅghârâma, 'gardens of the assembly,' originally denoting only 'the surrounding park, but afterwards transferred to the whole of the premises' (E. H., p. 118). Gomati, the name of this monastery, means 'rich in cows.'

are called to their meals by the sound of a bell. When they enter the refectory, their demeanour is marked by a reverent gravity, and they take their seats in regular order, all maintaining a perfect silence. No sound is heard from their alms-bowls and other utensils. When any of these pure men[1] require food, they are not allowed to call out (to the attendants) for it, but only make signs with their hands.

Hwuy-king, Tâo-ching, and Hwuy-tah set out in advance towards the country of K'eeh-ch'â[2]; but Fâ-hien and the others, wishing to see the procession of images, remained behind for three months. There are in this country four[3] great monasteries, not counting the smaller ones. Beginning on the first day of the fourth month, they sweep and water the streets inside the city, making a grand display in the lanes and byways. Over the city gate they pitch a large tent, grandly adorned in all possible ways, in which the king and queen, with their ladies brilliantly arrayed[4], take up their residence (for the time).

The monks of the Gomati monastery, being mahâyâna students, and held in greatest reverence by the king, took precedence of all the others in the procession. At a distance of three or four le from the city, they made a four-wheeled image car, more than thirty cubits high, which looked like the great hall (of a monastery) moving along. The seven precious substances[5] were grandly displayed about it, with silken streamers and

---

[1] A denomination for the monks as vimala, 'undefiled' or 'pure.' Giles makes it 'the menials that attend on the monks,' but I have not met with it in that application.

[2] K'eeh-ch'â has not been clearly identified. Rémusat made it Cashmere; Klaproth, Iskardu; Beal makes it Kartchou; and Eitel, Khas'a, 'an ancient tribe on the Paropamisus, the Kasioi of Ptolemy.' I think it was Ladak, or some well-known place in it. Hwuy-tah, unless that name be an alias, appears here for the first time.

[3] Instead of 'four,' the Chinese copies of the text have 'fourteen;' but the Corean reading is, probably, more correct.

[4] There may have been, as Giles says, 'maids of honour;' but the character does not say so.

[5] The Sapta-ratna, gold, silver, lapis lazuli, rock crystal, rubies, diamonds

canopies hanging all around. The (chief) image[1] stood in the middle of the car, with two Bodhisattvas[2] in attendance on it, while devas[3] were made to follow in waiting, all brilliantly carved in gold and silver, and hanging in the air. When (the car) was a hundred paces from the gate, the king put off his crown of state, changed his dress for a fresh suit, and with bare feet, carrying in his hands flowers and incense, and with two rows of attending followers, went out at the gate to meet the image; and, with his head and face (bowed to the ground), he did homage at its feet, and then scattered the flowers and burnt the incense. When the image was entering the gate, the queen and the brilliant ladies with her in the gallery above scattered far and wide all kinds of flowers, which floated about and fell promiscuously to the ground. In this way everything was done to promote the dignity of the occasion. The carriages of the monasteries were all different, and each one had its own day for the procession. (The ceremony) began on the first day of the fourth month, and ended on the fourteenth, after which the king and queen returned to the palace.

Seven or eight le to the west of the city there is what is called the King's New monastery, the building of which took eighty years, and extended over three reigns. It may be 250 cubits in height, rich in elegant

---

or emeralds, and agate. See Sacred Books of the East (Davids' Buddhist Suttas), vol. xi, p. 249.

[1] No doubt that of Śâkyamuni himself.

[2] A Bodhisattva is one whose essence has become intelligence; a Being who will in some future birth as a man (not necessarily or usually the next) attain to Buddhahood. The name does not include those Buddhas who have not yet attained to parinirvâṇa. The symbol of the state is an elephant fording a river. Popularly, its abbreviated form P'û-sâ is used in China for any idol or image; here the name has its proper signification.

[3] 諸天, 'all the thien,' or simply 'the thien' taken as plural. But in Chinese the character called thien (天) denotes heaven, or Heaven, and is interchanged with Tî and Shang Tî, meaning God. With the Buddhists it denotes the devas or Brahmanic gods, or all the inhabitants of the six devalokas. The usage shows the antagonism between Buddhism and Brahmanism, and still more that between it and Confucianism.

carving and inlaid work, covered above with gold and silver, and finished throughout with a combination of all the precious substances. Behind the tope there has been built a Hall of Buddha [1], of the utmost magnificence and beauty, the beams, pillars, venetianed doors, and windows being all overlaid with gold-leaf. Besides this, the apartments for the monks are imposingly and elegantly decorated, beyond the power of words to express. Of whatever things of highest value and preciousness the kings in the six countries on the east of the (Ts'ung) range of mountains [2] are possessed, they contribute the greater portion (to this monastery), using but a small portion of them themselves [3].

---

[1] Giles and Williams call this 'the oratory of Buddha.' But 'oratory' gives the idea of a small apartment, whereas the name here leads the mind to think of a large 'hall.' I once accompanied the monks of a large monastery from their refectory to the Hall of Buddha, which was a lofty and spacious apartment splendidly fitted up.

[2] The Ts'ung, or 'Onion' range, called also the Belurtagh mountains, including the Karakorùm, and forming together the connecting links between the more northern T'een-shan and the Kwun-lun mountains on the north of Thibet. It would be difficult to name the six countries which Fâ-hien had in mind.

[3] This seems to be the meaning here. My first impression of it was that the author meant to say that the contributions which they received were spent by the monks mainly on the buildings, and only to a small extent for themselves; and I still hesitate between that view and the one in the version.

There occurs here the binomial phrase kung-yang (供養), which is one of the most common throughout the narrative, and is used not only of support in the way of substantial contributions given to monks, monasteries, and Buddhism, but generally of all Buddhistic worship, if I may use that term in the connexion. Let me here quote two or three sentences from Davids' Manual (pp. 168–170):—'The members of the order are secured from want. There is no place in the Buddhist scheme for churches; the offering of flowers before the sacred tree or image of the Buddha takes the place of worship. Buddhism does not acknowledge the efficacy of prayers; and in the warm countries where Buddhists live, the occasional reading of the law, or preaching of the word, in public, can take place best in the open air, by moonlight, under a simple roof of trees or palms. There are five principal kinds of meditation, which in Buddhism takes the place of prayer.'

CHAPTER IV.

THROUGH THE TS'UNG OR 'ONION' MOUNTAINS TO K'EEH-CH'Â;—PROBABLY SKARDO, OR SOME CITY MORE TO THE EAST IN LADAK.

WHEN the processions of images in the fourth month were over, Săng-shâo, by himself alone, followed a Tartar who was an earnest follower of the Law[1], and proceeded towards Kophene[2]. Fâ-hien and the others went forward to the kingdom of Tsze-hoh, which it took them twenty-five days to reach[3]. Its king was a strenuous follower of our Law[4], and had (around him) more than a thousand monks, mostly students of the mahâyâna. Here (the travellers) abode fifteen days, and then went south for four days, when they found themselves among the Ts'ung-ling mountains, and reached the country of Yu-hwuy[5], where they

---

[1] This Tartar is called a 道人, 'a man of the Tâo,' or faith of Buddha. It occurs several times in the sequel, and denotes the man who is not a Buddhist outwardly only, but inwardly as well, whose faith is always making itself manifest in his ways. The name may be used of followers of other systems of faith besides Buddhism.

[2] See the account of the kingdom of Kophene, in the 96th Book of the first Han Records, p. 78, where its capital is said to be 12,200 le from Ch'ang-gan. It was the whole or part of the present Cabulistan. The name of Cophene is connected with the river Kophes, supposed to be the same as the present Cabul river, which falls into the Indus, from the west, at Attock, after passing Peshâwur. The city of Cabul, the capital of Afghanistan, may be the Kophene of the text; but we do not know that Săng-shâo and his guide got so far west. The text only says that they set out from Khoten 'towards it.'

[3] Tsze-hoh has not been identified. Beal thinks it was Yarkand, which, however, was north-west from Khoten. Watters ('China Review,' p. 135) rather approves the suggestion of 'Tashkurgan in Sirikul' for it. As it took Fâ-hien twenty-five days to reach it, it must have been at least 150 miles from Khoten.

[4] The king is described here by a Buddhistic phrase, denoting the possession of vîryabala, 'the power of energy; persevering exertion—one of the five moral powers' (E. H., p. 170).

[5] Nor has Yu-hwuy been clearly identified. Evidently it was directly south from

halted and kept their retreat [1]. When this was over, they went on among the hills [2] for twenty-five days, and got to K'eeh-ch'â [3], there rejoining Hwuy-king [4] and his two companions.

CHAPTER V.

GREAT QUINQUENNIAL ASSEMBLY OF MONKS. RELICS OF BUDDHA. PRODUCTIONS OF THE COUNTRY.

IT happened that the king of the country was then holding the pañcha parishad, that is, in Chinese, the great quinquennial assembly [5]. When this is to be held, the king requests the presence of the Śramans from all quarters (of his kingdom). They come (as if) in clouds; and when they are all assembled, their place of session is grandly decorated. Silken streamers and canopies are hung out in it, and water-lilies in gold and silver are made and fixed up behind the places where (the chief of them) are to sit. When clean mats have been spread, and they are all seated, the king and his ministers present their offerings according to rule and law. (The assembly takes place), in the first, second, or third month, for the most part in the spring.

Tsze-hoh, and among the 'Onion' mountains. Watters hazards the conjecture that it was the Aktasch of our present maps.

[1] This was the retreat already twice mentioned as kept by the pilgrims in the summer, the different phraseology, 'quiet rest,' without any mention of the season, indicating their approach to India, E. H., p. 168. Two, if not three, years had elapsed since they left Ch'ang-gan. Are we now with them in 402?

[2] This is the Corean reading (山), much preferable to the 止 of the Chinese editions.

[3] See p. 18, note 2. Watters approves of Klaproth's determination of K'eeh-ch'â to be Iskardu or Skardo. There are difficulties in connexion with the view, but it has the advantage, to my mind very great, of bringing the pilgrims across the Indus. The passage might be accomplished with ease at this point of the river's course, and therefore is not particularly mentioned.

[4] Who had preceded them from Khoten, p. 18.

[5] See Eitel, p. 89. He describes the assembly as 'an ecclesiastical conference, first instituted by king Aśoka for general confession of sins and inculcation of morality.'

After the king has held the assembly, he further exhorts the ministers to make other and special offerings. The doing of this extends over one, two, three, five, or even seven days; and when all is finished, he takes his own riding-horse, saddles, bridles, and waits on him himself[1], while he makes the noblest and most important minister of the kingdom mount him. Then, taking fine white woollen cloth, all sorts of precious things, and articles which the Śramans require, he distributes them among them, uttering vows at the same time along with all his ministers; and when this distribution has taken place, he again redeems (whatever he wishes) from the monks[2].

The country, being among the hills and cold, does not produce the other cereals, and only the wheat gets ripe. After the monks have received their annual (portion of this), the mornings suddenly show the hoar-frost, and on this account the king always begs the monks to make the wheat ripen[3] before they receive their portion. There is in the country a spittoon which belonged to Buddha, made of stone, and in colour like his alms-bowl. There is also a tooth of Buddha, for which the people have reared a tope, connected with which there are more than a thousand monks and their disciples[4], all students of the hînayâna. To the east of these hills the dress of the common people is of coarse materials, as in our country of Ts'in, but here also[5] there were among them the differences of fine woollen cloth and of serge or haircloth. The rules observed by the Śramans are remarkable, and too numerous to be mentioned in detail. The country is in the midst of the Onion range.

---

[1] The text of this sentence is perplexing; and all translators, including myself, have been puzzled by it.

[2] See what we are told of king Aśoka's grant of all the Jambudvîpa to the monks in chapter xxvii. There are several other instances of similar gifts in the Mahâvaṇsa.

[3] Watters calls attention to this as showing that the monks of K'eeh-ch'â had the credit of possessing weather-controlling powers.

[4] The text here has 僧徒, not 僧 alone. I often found in monasteries boys and lads who looked up to certain of the monks as their preceptors.

[5] Compare what is said in chapter ii of the dress of the people of Shen-shen.

As you go forward from these mountains, the plants, trees, and fruits are all different from those of the land of Han, excepting only the bamboo, pomegranate[1], and sugar-cane.

CHAPTER VI.

ON TOWARDS NORTH INDIA. DARADA. IMAGE OF MAITREYA BODHISATTVA.

FROM this (the travellers) went westwards towards North India, and after being on the way for a month, they succeeded in getting across and through the range of the Onion mountains. The snow rests on them both winter and summer. There are also among them venomous dragons, which, when provoked, spit forth poisonous winds, and cause showers of snow and storms of sand and gravel. Not one in ten thousand of those who encounter these dangers escapes with his life. The people of the country call the range by the name of 'The Snow mountains.' When (the travellers) had got through them, they were in North India, and immediately on entering its borders, found themselves in a small kingdom called T'o-leih[2], where also there were many monks, all students of the hînayâna.

In this kingdom there was formerly an Arhan[3], who by his supernatural

---

[1] Giles thinks the fruit here was the guava, because the ordinary name for 'pomegranate' is preceded by gan (安); but the pomegranate was called at first Gan Shih-lâu, as having been introduced into China from Gan-seih by Chang K'een, who is referred to in chapter vii.

[2] Eitel and others identify this with Darada, the country of the ancient Dardae, the region near Dardus; lat. 30° 11′ N., lon. 73° 54′ E. See E. H., p. 30. I am myself in more than doubt on the point. Cunningham ('Ancient Geography of India,' p. 82) says, 'Darel is a valley on the right or western bank of the Indus, now occupied by Dardus or Dards, from whom it received its name.' But as I read our narrative, Fâ-hien is here on the eastern bank of the Indus, and only crosses to the western bank as described in the next chapter.

[3] Lo-han, Arhat, Arahat are all designations of the perfected Ârya, the disciple who has passed the different stages of the Noble Path, or eightfold

power[1] took a clever artificer up to the Tushita[2] heaven, to see the height, complexion, and appearance of Maitreya Bodhisattva[3], and then return and make an image of him in wood. First and last, this was done three times, and then the image was completed, eighty cubits in height, and eight cubits at the base from knee to knee of the crossed legs. On fast-days it emits an effulgent light. The kings of the (surrounding) countries vie with one another in presenting offerings to it. Here it is,—to be seen now as of old[4].

---

excellent way, who has conquered all passions, and is not to be reborn again. Arhatship implies possession of certain supernatural powers, and is not to be succeeded by Buddhaship, but implies the fact of the saint having already attained nirvâṇa. Popularly, the Chinese designate by this name the wider circle of Buddha's disciples, as well as the smaller ones of 500 and 18. No temple in Canton is better worth a visit than that of the 500 Lo-han.

[1] Ṛiddhi-sâkshâtkriyâ, 'the power of supernatural footsteps,'='a body flexible at pleasure,' or unlimited power over the body. E. H., p. 104.

[2] Tushita is the fourth Devaloka, where all Bodhisattvas are reborn before finally appearing on earth as Buddha. Life lasts in Tushita 4000 years, but twenty-four hours there are equal to 400 years on earth. E. H., p. 152.

[3] Maitreya (Spence Hardy, Maitri), often styled Ajita, 'the Invincible,' was a Bodhisattva, the principal one, indeed, of Śâkyamuni's retinue, but is not counted among the ordinary (historical) disciples, nor is anything told of his antecedents. It was in the Tushita heaven that Śâkyamuni met him and appointed him as his successor, to appear as Buddha after the lapse of 5000 years. Maitreya is therefore the expected Messiah of the Buddhists, residing at present in Tushita, and, according to the account of him in Eitel (H., p. 70), 'already controlling the propagation of the Buddhistic faith.' The name means 'gentleness' or 'kindness;' and this will be the character of his dispensation.

[4] The combination of 今故 in the text of this concluding sentence, and so frequently occurring throughout the narrative, has occasioned no little dispute among previous translators. In the imperial thesaurus of phraseology (P'ei-wăn Yun-foo), under 故, an example of it is given from Chwang-tsze, and a note subjoined that 今故 is equivalent to 古今, 'anciently and now.'

CHAPTER VII.

CROSSING OF THE INDUS. WHEN BUDDHISM FIRST CROSSED THE RIVER FOR THE EAST.

THE travellers went on to the south-west for fifteen days (at the foot of the mountains, and) following the course of their range. The way was difficult and rugged, (running along) a bank exceedingly precipitous, which rose up there, a hill-like wall of rock, 10,000 cubits from the base. When one approached the edge of it, his eyes became unsteady; and if he wished to go forward in the same direction, there was no place on which he could place his foot; and beneath were the waters of the river called the Indus[1]. In former times men had chiselled paths along the rocks, and distributed ladders on the face of them, to the number altogether of 700, at the bottom of which there was a suspension bridge of ropes, by which the river was crossed, its banks being there eighty paces apart[2]. The (place and arrangements) are to be found in the Records of the Nine Interpreters[3],

---

[1] The Sindhu. We saw in a former note (2, p. 14), that the earliest name in China for India was Shin-tuh. So, here, the river Indus is called by a name approaching that in sound.

[2] Both Beal and Watters quote from Cunningham (Ladak, pp. 88, 89) the following description of the course of the Indus in these parts, in striking accordance with our author's account:—'From Skardo to Rongdo, and from Rongdo to Makpou-i-shang-rong, for upwards of 100 miles, the Indus sweeps sullen and dark through a mighty gorge in the mountains, which for wild sublimity is perhaps unequalled. Rongdo means the country of defiles . . . . Between these points the Indus raves from side to side of the gloomy chasm, foaming and chafing with ungovernable fury. Yet even in these inaccessible places has daring and ingenious man triumphed over opposing nature. The yawning abyss is spanned by frail rope bridges, and the narrow ledges of rocks are connected by ladders to form a giddy pathway overhanging the seething caldron below.'

[3] The Japanese edition has a different reading here from the Chinese copies,—one which Rémusat (with true critical instinct) conjectured should take the place of the more difficult text with which alone he was acquainted. The 'Nine Interpreters' would be a general name for the official interpreters

but neither Chang K'een[1] nor Kan Ying[2] had reached the spot.

The monks[3] asked Fâ-hien if it could be known when the Law of Buddha first went to the east. He replied, 'When I asked the people of those countries about it, they all said that it had been handed down by their fathers from of old that, after the setting up of the image of Maitreya Bodhisattva, there were Śramans of India who crossed this river, carrying with them Sûtras and Books of Discipline. Now the image was set up rather more than 300 years after the nirvâṇa[4] of Buddha, which may be referred to the reign of king P'ing of the Chow dynasty[5]. According

---

attached to the invading armies of Han in their attempts to penetrate and subdue the regions of the west. The phrase occurs in the memoir of Chang K'een, referred to in the next note.

[1] Chang K'een, a minister of the emperor Woo of Han (B.C. 140–87), is celebrated as the first Chinese who 'pierced the void,' and penetrated to 'the regions of the west,' corresponding very much to the present Turkestan. Through him, by B.C. 115, a regular intercourse was established between China and the thirty-six kingdoms or states of that quarter;—see Mayers' Chinese Reader's Manual, p. 5. The memoir of Chang K'een, translated by Mr. Wylie from the Books of the first Han dynasty, appears in the Journal of the Anthropological Institute, referred to already (note 3, p. 12).

[2] Less is known of Kan Ying than of Chang K'een. Being sent in A.D. 88 by his patron Pan Châo on an embassy to the Roman empire, he only got as far as the Caspian sea, and returned to China. He extended, however, the knowledge of his countrymen with regard to the western regions;—see the memoir of Pan Châo in the Books of the second Han, and Mayers' Manual, pp. 167, 168.

[3] Where and when? Probably at his first resting-place after crossing the Indus.

[4] This may refer to Śâkyamuni's becoming Buddha on attaining to nirvâṇa, or more probably to his pari-nirvâṇa and death.

[5] As king P'ing's reign lasted from B.C. 750 to 719, this would place the death of Buddha in the eleventh century B.C., whereas recent inquirers place it between B.C. 480 and 470, a year or two, or a few years, after that of Confucius, so that the two great 'Masters' of the east were really contemporaries. But if Rhys Davids be correct, as I think he is, in fixing the date of Buddha's death

to this account we may say that the diffusion of our great doctrines (in the east) began from (the setting up of) this image. If it had not been through that Maitreya[1], the great spiritual master[2] (who is to be) the successor of the Śâkya, who could have caused the "Three Precious Ones[3]" to be proclaimed so far, and the people of those border lands to know our Law? We know of a truth that the opening of (the way for such) a mysterious propagation is not the work of man; and so the dream of the emperor Ming of Han[4] had its proper cause.'

CHAPTER VIII.

WOO-CHANG, OR UDYÂNA. MONASTERIES, AND THEIR WAYS. TRACES OF BUDDHA.

AFTER crossing the river, (the travellers) immediately came to the kingdom of Woo-chang[5], which is indeed (a part) of North India. The people all use the language of Central India, 'Central India' being what we should call the 'Middle Kingdom.' The food and clothes of the common people are the same as in that Central Kingdom. The Law of Buddha is very (flourishing in Woo-chang). They call the places where the monks stay (for a time) or reside permanently Saṅghârâmas[6]; and of these there are in all 500, the monks being all students of the

---

within a few years of 412 B.C. (see Manual, p. 213), not to speak of Westergaard's still lower date, then the Buddha was very considerably the junior of Confucius.

[1] This confirms the words of Eitel (note 3, p. 23), that Maitreya is already controlling the propagation of the Faith.

[2] The Chinese characters for this simply mean 'the great scholar or officer;' but see Eitel's Handbook, p. 99, on the term purusha.

[3] 'The precious Buddha,' 'the precious Law,' and 'the precious Monkhood;' Buddha, Dharma, and Saṅgha; the whole being equivalent to Buddhism.

[4] Fâ-hien thus endorses the view that Buddhism was introduced into China in this reign, A.D. 58–75. The emperor had his dream in A.D. 61.

[5] Udyâna, meaning 'the Park;' just north of the Punjâb, the country along the Subhavastu, now called the Swat; noted for its forests, flowers, and fruits (E. H., p. 153).

[6] See note 3, p. 17.

hînayâna. When stranger bhikshus[1] arrive at one of them, their wants are supplied for three days, after which they are told to find a resting-place for themselves.

There is a tradition that when Buddha came to North India, he came at once to this country, and that here he left a print of his foot, which is long or short according to the ideas of the beholder (on the subject). It exists, and the same thing is true about it, at the present day. Here also are still to be seen the rock on which he dried his clothes, and the place where he converted the wicked dragon[2]. The rock is fourteen cubits high, and more than twenty broad, with one side of it smooth.

Hwuy-king, Hwuy-tah, and Tâo-ching went on ahead towards (the place of) Buddha's shadow in the country of Nâgara[3]; but Fâ-hien and the others remained in Woo-chang, and kept the summer retreat[4]. That over, they descended south, and arrived in the country of Soo-ho-to[5].

---

[1] Bhikshu is the name for a monk as 'living by alms,' a mendicant. All bhikshus call themselves Śramans. Sometimes the two names are used together by our author.

[2] Nâga is the Sanskrit name for the Chinese lung or dragon; often meaning a snake, especially the boa. 'Chinese Buddhists,' says Eitel, p. 79, 'when speaking of nâgas as boa spirits, always represent them as enemies of mankind, but when viewing them as deities of rivers, lakes, or oceans, they describe them as piously inclined.' The dragon, however, is in China the symbol of the Sovereign and Sage, a use of it unknown in Buddhism, according to which all nâgas need to be converted in order to obtain a higher phase of being. The use of the character too (度), as here, in the sense of 'to convert,' is entirely Buddhistic. The six pâramitâs are the six virtues which carry men across (度) the great sea of life and death, as the sphere of transmigration to nirvâṇa. With regard to the particular conversion here, Eitel (p. 11) says the Nâga's name was Apatâla, the guardian deity of the Subhavastu river, and that he was converted by Śâkyamuni shortly before the death of the latter.

[3] In Chinese. Na-k'eeh, an ancient kingdom and city on the southern bank of the Cabul river, about thirty miles west of Jellalabad.

[4] We would seem now to be in 403.

[5] Soo-ho-to has not been clearly identified. Beal says that later Buddhist writers include it in Udyâna. It must have been between the Indus and the Swat. I suppose it was what we now call Swastene.

CHAPTER IX.

SOO-HO-TO. LEGEND OF BUDDHA.

IN that country also Buddhism[1] is flourishing. There is in it the place where Śakra[2], Ruler of Devas, in a former age[3], tried the Bodhisattva, by producing[4] a hawk (in pursuit of a) dove, when (the Bodhi-

---

[1] Buddhism stands for the two Chinese characters 佛法, 'the Law of Buddha,' and to that rendering of the phrase, which is of frequent occurrence, I will in general adhere. Buddhism is not an adequate rendering of them any more than Christianity would be of τὸ εὐαγγέλιον Χριστοῦ. The Fâ or Law is the equivalent of dharma comprehending all in the first Basket of the Buddhist teaching,—as Dr. Davids says (Hibbert Lectures, p. 44), 'its ethics and philosophy, and its system of self-culture;' with the theory of karma, it seems to me, especially underlying it. It has been pointed out (Cunningham's 'Bhilsa Topes,' p. 102) that dharma is the keystone of all king Priyadarśi or Aśoka's edicts. The whole of them are dedicated to the attainment of one object, 'the advancement of dharma, or of the Law of Buddha.' His native Chinese afforded no better character than 法 or Law, by which our author could express concisely his idea of the Buddhistic system, as 'a law of life,' a directory or system of Rules, by which men could attain to the consummation of their being.

[2] Śakra is a common name for the Brahmanic Indra, adopted by Buddhism into the circle of its own great adherents;—it has been said, 'because of his popularity.' He is generally styled, as here, T'een Tî, 'God or Ruler of Devas.' He is now the representative of the secular power, the valiant protector of the Buddhist body, but is looked upon as inferior to Śâkyamuni, and every Buddhist saint. He appears several times in Fâ-hien's narrative. E. H., pp. 108 and 46.

[3] The Chinese character is 昔, 'formerly,' and is often, as in the first sentence of the narrative, simply equivalent to that adverb. At other times it means, as here, 'in a former age,' some pre-existent state in the time of a former birth. The incident related is 'a Jâtaka story.'

[4] It occurs at once to a translator to render the characters 化作 by 'changed himself to.' Such is often their meaning in the sequel, but their use in chapter xxiv

sattva) cut off a piece of his own flesh, and (with it) ransomed the dove. After Buddha had attained to perfect wisdom[1], and in travelling about with his disciples (arrived at this spot), he informed them that this was the place where he ransomed the dove with a piece of his own flesh. In this way the people of the country became aware of the fact, and on the spot reared a tope, adorned with layers[2] of gold and silver plates.

CHAPTER X.

GANDHÂRA. LEGENDS OF BUDDHA.

THE travellers, going downwards from this towards the east, in five days came to the country of Gandhâra[3], the place where Dharma-vivardhana[4], the son of Aśoka[5], ruled. When Buddha was a Bodhisattva, he gave his eyes also for another man here[6]; and at the spot they have

---

may be considered as a crucial test of the meaning which I have given to them here.

[1] That is, had become Buddha, or completed his course (成道).

[2] This seems to be the contribution of 校 (or 挍), to the force of the binomial 校飾, which is continually occurring.

[3] Eitel says 'an ancient kingdom, corresponding to the region about Dheri and Banjour.' But see note 1 on next page.

[4] Dharma-vivardhana is the name in Sanskrit, represented by the Fâ Yî (法益) of the text.

[5] Aśoka is here mentioned for the first time;—the Constantine of the Buddhist society, and famous for the number of vihâras and topes which he erected. He was the grandson of Chandragupta (i.q. Sandracottus), a rude adventurer, who at one time was a refugee in the camp of Alexander the Great; and within about twenty years afterwards drove the Greeks out of India, having defeated Seleucus, the Greek ruler of the Indus provinces. He had by that time made himself king of Magadha. His grandson was converted to Buddhism by the bold and patient demeanour of an Arhat whom he had ordered to be buried alive, and became a most zealous supporter of the new faith. Dr. Rhys Davids (Sacred Books of the East, vol. xi, p. xlvi) says that 'Aśoka's coronation can be fixed with absolute certainty within a year or two either way of 267 B.C.'

[6] This also is a Jâtaka story; but Eitel thinks it may be a myth, constructed from the story of the blinding of Dharma-vivardhana.

also reared a large tope, adorned with layers of gold and silver plates. The people of the country were mostly students of the hînayâna.

CHAPTER XI.

TAKSHAŚILÂ. LEGENDS. THE FOUR GREAT TOPES.

SEVEN days' journey from this to the east brought the travellers to the kingdom of Takshaśilâ[1], which means 'the severed head' in the language of China. Here, when Buddha was a Bodhisattva, he gave away his head to a man[2]; and from this circumstance the kingdom got its name.

Going on further for two days to the east, they came to the place where the Bodhisattva threw down his body to feed a starving tigress[2]. In these two places also large topes have been built, both adorned with layers of all the precious substances. The kings, ministers, and peoples of the kingdoms around vie with one another in making offerings at them. The trains of those who come to scatter flowers and light lamps at them never cease. The nations of those quarters call those (and the other two mentioned before) 'the four great topes.'

---

[1] See Julien's 'Méthode pour déchiffrer et transcrire les Noms Sanscrits,' p. 206. Eitel says, 'The Taxila of the Greeks, the region near Hoosun Abdaul in lat. 35° 48′ N., lon. 72° 44′ E. But this identification, I am satisfied, is wrong. Cunningham, indeed, takes credit ('Ancient Geography of India,' pp. 108, 109) for determining this to be the site of Arrian's Taxila,—in the upper Punjâb, still existing in the ruins of Shahdheri, between the Indus and Hydaspes (the modern Jhelum). So far he may be correct; but the Takshaśilâ of Fâ-hien was on the other, or western side of the Indus; and between the river and Gandhâra. It took him, indeed, seven days travelling eastwards to reach it; but we do not know what stoppages he may have made on the way. We must be wary in reckoning distances from his specifications of days.

[2] Two Jâtaka stories. See the account of the latter in Spence Hardy's 'Manual of Buddhism,' pp. 91, 92. It took place when Buddha had been born as a Brahman in the village of Daliddi; and from the merit of the act, he was next born in a devaloka.

CHAPTER XII.

PURUSHAPURA, OR PESHÂWUR. PROPHECY ABOUT KING KANISHKA AND HIS TOPE. BUDDHA'S ALMS-BOWL. DEATH OF HWUY-YING.

GOING southwards from Gândhâra, (the travellers) in four days arrived at the kingdom of Purushapura[1]. Formerly, when Buddha was travelling in this country with his disciples, he said to Ânanda[2], 'After my pari-nirvâṇa[3], there will be a king named Kanishka[4], who shall on this spot build a tope.' This Kanishka was afterwards born into the world; and (once), when he had gone forth to look about him,

---

[1] The modern Peshâwur, lat. 34° 8′ N., lon. 71° 30′ E.

[2] A first cousin of Śâkyamuni, and born at the moment when he attained to Buddhaship. Under Buddha's teaching, Ânanda became an Arhat, and is famous for his strong and accurate memory; and he played an important part at the first council for the formation of the Buddhist canon. The friendship between Śâkyamuni and Ânanda was very close and tender; and it is impossible to read much of what the dying Buddha said to him and of him, as related in the Mahâ-pari-nirvâṇa Sûtra, without being moved almost to tears. Ânanda is to reappear on earth as Buddha in another Kalpa. See E. H., p. 9, and the Sacred Books of the East, vol. xi.

[3] On his attaining to nirvâṇa, Śâkyamuni became the Buddha, and had no longer to mourn his being within the circle of transmigration, and could rejoice in an absolute freedom from passion, and a perfect purity. Still he continued to live on for forty-five years, till he attained to pari-nirvâṇa, and had done with all the life of sense and society, and had no more exercise of thought. He died; but whether he absolutely and entirely ceased to be, in any sense of the word being, it would be difficult to say. Probably he himself would not and could not have spoken definitely on the point. So far as our use of language is concerned, apart from any assured faith in and hope of immortality, his pari-nirvâṇa was his death.

[4] Kanishka appeared, and began to reign, early in our first century, about A.D. 10. He was the last of three brothers, whose original seat was in Yüeh-she, immediately mentioned, or Tukhâra. Converted by the sudden appearance of a saint, he became a zealous Buddhist, and patronised the system as liberally as Aśoka had done. The finest topes in the north-west of India are ascribed to him; he was certainly a great man and a magnificent sovereign.

Śakra, Ruler of Devas, wishing to excite the idea in his mind, assumed the appearance of a little herd-boy, and was making a tope right in the way (of the king), who asked what sort of a thing he was making. The boy said, 'I am making a tope for Buddha.' The king said, 'Very good;' and immediately, right over the boy's tope, he (proceeded to) rear another, which was more than four hundred cubits high, and adorned with layers of all the precious substances. Of all the topes and temples which (the travellers) saw in their journeyings, there was not one comparable to this in solemn beauty and majestic grandeur. There is a current saying that this is the finest tope in Jambudvîpa[1]. When the king's tope was completed, the little tope (of the boy) came out from its side on the south, rather more than three cubits in height.

Buddha's alms-bowl is in this country. Formerly, a king of Yüeh-she[2] raised a large force and invaded this country, wishing to carry the bowl away. Having subdued the kingdom, as he and his captains were sincere believers in the Law of Buddha, and wished to carry off the bowl, they proceeded to present their offerings on a great scale. When they had done so to the Three Precious Ones, he made a large elephant be grandly caparisoned, and placed the bowl upon it. But the elephant knelt down on the ground, and was unable to go forward. Again he caused a four-wheeled waggon to be prepared in which the bowl was put to be conveyed away. Eight elephants were then yoked to it, and dragged it with their united strength; but neither were they able to

---

[1] Jambudvîpa is one of the four great continents of the universe, representing the inhabited world as fancied by the Buddhists, and so called because it resembles in shape the leaves of the jambu tree. It is south of mount Meru, and divided among four fabulous kings (E. H., p. 36). It is often used, as here perhaps, merely as the Buddhist name for India.

[2] This king was perhaps Kanishka himself, Fâ-hien mixing up, in an inartistic way, different legends about him. Eitel suggests that a relic of the old name of the country may still exist in that of the Jats or Juts of the present day. A more common name for it is Tukhâra, and he observes that the people were the Indo-Scythians of the Greeks, and the Tartars of Chinese writers, who, driven on by the Huns (180 B.C.), conquered Transoxiana, destroyed the Bactrian kingdom (126 B.C.), and finally conquered the Punjâb, Cashmere, and great part of India, their greatest king being Kanishka (E. H., p. 152).

go forward. The king knew that the time for an association between himself and the bowl had not yet arrived[1], and was sad and deeply ashamed of himself. Forthwith he built a tope at the place and a monastery, and left a guard to watch (the bowl), making all sorts of contributions.

There may be there more than seven hundred monks. When it is near midday, they bring out the bowl, and, along with the common people[2], make their various offerings to it, after which they take their midday meal. In the evening, at the time of incense, they bring the bowl out again[3]. It may contain rather more than two pecks, and is of various colours, black predominating, with the seams that show its fourfold composition distinctly marked[4]. Its thickness is about the fifth of an inch, and it has a bright and glossy lustre. When poor people throw into it a few flowers, it becomes immediately full, while some very rich people, wishing to make offering of many flowers, might not stop till they had thrown in hundreds, thousands, and myriads of bushels, and yet would not be able to fill it[5].

---

[1] Watters, clearly understanding the thought of the author in this sentence, renders—'his destiny did not extend to a connexion with the bowl;' but the term 'destiny' suggests a controlling or directing power without. The king thought that his virtue in the past was not yet sufficient to give him possession of the bowl.

[2] The text is simply 'those in white clothes.' This may mean 'the laity,' or the '**upâsakas**;' but it is better to take the characters in their common Chinese acceptation, as meaning 'commoners,' 'men who have no rank.' See in Williams' Dictionary under 白.

[3] I do not wonder that Rémusat should give for this—'et s'en retournent après.' But Fâ-hien's use of 爾 in the sense of 'in the same way' is uniform throughout the narrative.

[4] Hardy's M. B., p. 183, says:—'The alms-bowl, given by Mahâbrahma, having vanished (about the time that Gotama became Buddha), each of the four guardian deities brought him an alms-bowl of emerald, but he did not accept them. They then brought four bowls made of stone, of the colour of the mung fruit; and when each entreated that his own bowl might be accepted, Buddha caused them to appear as if formed into a single bowl, appearing at the upper rim as if placed one within the other.' See the account more correctly given in the 'Buddhist Birth Stories,' p. 110.

[5] Compare the narrative in Luke's Gospel, xxi. 1–4.

Pâo-yun and Săng-king here merely made their offerings to the alms-bowl, and (then resolved to) go back. Hwuy-king, Hwuy-tah, and Tâo-ching had gone on before the rest to Nagâra[1], to make their offerings at (the places of) Buddha's shadow, tooth, and the flat-bone of his skull. (There) Hwuy-king fell ill, and Tâo-ching remained to look after him, while Hwuy-tah came alone to Purushapura, and saw the others, and (then) he with Pâo-yun and Săng-king took their way back to the land of Ts'in. Hwuy-king[2] came to his end[3] in the monastery of Buddha's alms-bowl, and on this Fâ-hien went forward alone towards the place of the flat-bone of Buddha's skull.

CHAPTER XIII.

NAGÂRA. FESTIVAL OF BUDDHA'S SKULL-BONE. OTHER RELICS, AND HIS SHADOW.

GOING west for sixteen yojanas[4], he came to the city He-lo[5] in the borders of the country of Nagâra, where there is the flat-bone of Buddha's skull, deposited in a vihâra[6] adorned all over with gold-leaf

---

[1] See chapter viii.

[2] This, no doubt, should be Hwuy-ying. King was at this time ill in Nagâra, and indeed afterwards he dies in crossing the Little Snowy Mountains; but all the texts make him die twice. The confounding of the two names has been pointed out by Chinese critics.

[3] 'Came to his end;' i.e., according to the text, 'proved the impermanence and uncertainty,' namely, of human life. See Williams' Dictionary under 常. The phraseology is wholly Buddhistic.

[4] Now in India, Fâ-hien used the Indian measure of distance; but it is not possible to determine exactly what its length then was. The estimates of it are very different, and vary from four and a half or five miles to seven, and sometimes more. See the subject exhaustively treated in Davids' 'Ceylon Coins and Measures,' pp. 15–17.

[5] The present Hidda, west of Peshâwur, and five miles south of Jellalabad.

[6] 'The vihâra,' says Hardy, 'is the residence of a recluse or priest;' and so Davids:—'the clean little hut where the mendicant lives.' Our author, however, does not use the Indian name here, but the Chinese characters which express its meaning—tsing shay, 'a pure dwelling.' He uses the term occasionally, and

and the seven sacred substances. The king of the country, revering and honouring the bone, and anxious lest it should be stolen away, has selected eight individuals, representing the great families in the kingdom, and committed to each a seal, with which he should seal (its shrine) and guard (the relic). At early dawn these eight men come, and after each has inspected his seal, they open the door. This done, they wash their hands with scented water and bring out the bone, which they place outside the vihâra, on a lofty platform, where it is supported on a round pedestal of the seven precious substances, and covered with a bell of lapis lazuli, both adorned with rows of pearls. Its colour is of a yellowish white, and it forms an imperfect circle twelve inches round[1], curving upwards to the centre. Every day, after it has been brought forth, the keepers of the vihâra ascend a high gallery, where they beat great drums, blow conchs, and clash their copper cymbals. When the king hears them, he goes to the vihâra, and makes his offerings of flowers and incense. When he has done this, he (and his attendants) in order, one after another, (raise the bone), place it (for a moment) on the top of their heads[2], and then depart, going out by the door on the west as they had entered by that on the east. The king every morning makes his offerings and performs his worship, and afterwards gives

---

evidently, in this sense; more frequently it occurs in his narrative in connexion with the Buddhist relic worship; and at first I translated it by 'shrine' and 'shrine-house;' but I came to the conclusion, at last, to employ always the Indian name. The first time I saw a shrine-house was, I think, in a monastery near Foo-chow;—a small pyramidal structure, about ten feet high, glittering as if with the precious substances, but all, it seemed to me, of tinsel. It was in a large apartment of the building, having many images in it. The monks said it was the most precious thing in their possession, and that if they opened it, as I begged them to do, there would be a convulsion that would destroy the whole establishment. See E. H., p. 166. The name of the province of Behar was given to it in consequence of its many vihâras.

[1] According to the characters, 'square, round, four inches.' Hsüan-chwang says it was twelve inches round.

[2] In Williams' Dictionary, under 頂, the characters, used here, are employed in the phrase for 'to degrade an officer,' that is, 'to remove the token of his rank worn on the crown of his head;' but to place a thing on the crown is a Buddhistic form of religious homage.

audience on the business of his government. The chiefs of the Vaiśyas[1] also make their offerings before they attend to their family affairs. Every day it is so, and there is no remissness in the observance of the custom. When all the offerings are over, they replace the bone in the vihâra, where there is a vimoksha tope[2], of the seven precious substances, and rather more than five cubits high, sometimes open, sometimes shut, to contain it. In front of the door of the vihâra, there are parties who every morning sell flowers and incense[3], and those who wish to make offerings buy some of all kinds. The kings of various countries are also constantly sending messengers with offerings. The vihâra stands in a square of thirty paces, and though heaven should shake and earth be rent, this place would not move.

Going on, north from this, for a yojana, (Fâ-hien) arrived at the capital of Nagâra, the place where the Bodhisattva once purchased with money five stalks of flowers, as an offering to the Dîpâṅkara Buddha[4]. In the midst of the city there is also the tope of Buddha's tooth, where offerings are made in the same way as to the flat-bone of his skull.

A yojana to the north-east of the city brought him to the mouth of a valley, where there is Buddha's pewter staff[5]; and a vihâra also has

---

[1] The Vaiśyas, or bourgeois caste of Hindu society, are described here as 'resident scholars.'

[2] See Eitel's Handbook under the name vimoksha, which is explained as 'the act of self-liberation,' and 'the dwelling or state of liberty.' There are eight acts of liberating one's self from all subjective and objective trammels, and as many states of liberty (vimukti) resulting therefrom. They are eight degrees of self-inanition, and apparently eight stages on the way to nirvâṇa. The tope in the text would be emblematic in some way of the general idea of the mental progress conducting to the Buddhistic consummation of existence.

[3] This incense would be in long 'sticks,' small and large, such as are sold to-day throughout China, as you enter the temples.

[4] 'The illuminating Buddha,' the twenty-fourth predecessor of Śâkyamuni, and who, so long before, gave him the assurance that he would by-and-by be Buddha. See Jâtaka Tales, p. 23.

[5] The staff was, as immediately appears, of Gośîrsha Chandana, or 'sandal-wood from the Cow's-head mountain,' a species of copper-brown sandal-

been built at which offerings are made. The staff is made of Gośîrsha Chandana, and is quite sixteen or seventeen cubits long. It is contained in a wooden tube, and though a hundred or a thousand men were to (try to) lift it, they could not move it.

Entering the mouth of the valley, and going west, he found Buddha's Saṅghâli[1], where also there is reared a vihâra, and offerings are made. It is a custom of the country when there is a great drought, for the people to collect in crowds, bring out the robe, pay worship to it, and make offerings, on which there is immediately a great rain from the sky.

South of the city, half a yojana, there is a rock-cavern, in a great hill fronting the south-west; and here it was that Buddha left his shadow. Looking at it from a distance of more than ten paces, you seem to see Buddha's real form, with his complexion of gold, and his characteristic marks[2] in their nicety clearly and brightly displayed. The nearer you approach, however, the fainter it becomes, as if it were only in your fancy. When the kings from the regions all around have sent skilful artists to take a copy, none of them have been able to do so. Among the people of the country there is a saying current that 'the thousand Buddhas[3] must all leave their shadows here.'

Rather more than four hundred paces west from the shadow, when Buddha was at the spot, he shaved off his hair and clipt his nails, and proceeded, along with his disciples, to build a tope seventy or eighty

---

wood, said to be produced most abundantly on a mountain of (the fabulous continent) Ullarakuru, north of mount Meru, which resembles in shape the head of a cow (E. H., pp. 42, 43). It is called a 'pewter staff' from having on it a head and rings of pewter. See Watters, 'China Review,' viii, pp. 227, 228, and Williams' Dictionary, under 杖.

[1] Or Saṅghâṭi, the double or composite robe, part of a monk's attire, reaching from the shoulders to the knees, and fastened round the waist (E. H., p. 118).

[2] These were the 'marks and beauties' on the person of a supreme Buddha. The ṛishi Kalâ Devala saw them on the body of the infant Śâkya prince to the number of 328, those on the teeth, which had not yet come out, being visible to his spirit-like eyes (M. B., pp. 148, 149).

[3] Probably = 'all Buddhas.'

cubits high, to be a model for all future topes; and it is still existing. By the side of it there is a monastery, with more than seven hundred monks in it. At this place there are as many as a thousand topes[1] of Arhans and Pratyeka Buddhas[2].

CHAPTER XIV.

DEATH OF HWUY-KING IN THE LITTLE SNOWY MOUNTAINS. LO-E. POHNÂ. CROSSING THE INDUS TO THE EAST.

HAVING stayed there till the third month of winter, Fâ-hien and the two others[3], proceeding southwards, crossed the Little Snowy mountains[4]. On them the snow lies accumulated both winter and summer. On the north (side) of the mountains, in the shade, they suddenly encountered a cold wind which made them shiver and become unable to speak. Hwuy-king could not go any farther. A white froth came from his mouth,

---

[1] The number may appear too great. But see what is said on the size of topes in note 1, page 17.

[2] In Singhalese, Pasê Buddhas; called also Nidâna Buddhas, and Pratyeka Jinas, and explained by 'individually intelligent,' 'completely intelligent,' 'intelligent as regards the nidânas.' This, says Eitel (pp. 96, 97), is 'a degree of saintship unknown to primitive Buddhism, denoting automats in ascetic life who attain to Buddhaship "individually," that is, without a teacher, and without being able to save others. As the ideal hermit, the Pratyeka Buddha is compared with the rhinoceros khadga that lives lonely in the wilderness. He is also called Nidâna Buddha, as having mastered the twelve nidânas (the twelve links in the everlasting chain of cause and effect in the whole range of existence, the understanding of which solves the riddle of life, revealing the inanity of all forms of existence, and preparing the mind for nirvâṇa). He is also compared to a horse, which, crossing a river, almost buries its body under the water, without, however, touching the bottom of the river. Thus in crossing saṃsâra he "suppresses the errors of life and thought, and the effects of habit and passion, without attaining to absolute perfection."' Whether these Buddhas were unknown, as Eitel says, to primitive Buddhism, may be doubted. See Davids' Hibbert Lectures, p. 146.

[3] These must have been Tâo-ching and Hwuy-king.

[4] Probably the Safeid Koh, and on the way to the Kohat pass.

and he said to Fâ-hien, 'I cannot live any longer. Do you immediately go away, that we do not all die here;' and with these words he died[1]. Fâ-hien stroked the corpse, and cried out piteously, 'Our original plan has failed;—it is fate[2]. What can we do?' He then again exerted himself, and they succeeded in crossing to the south of the range, and arrived in the kingdom of Lo-e[3], where there were nearly three thousand monks, students of both the mahâyâna and hînayâna. Here they stayed for the summer retreat[4], and when that was over, they went on to the south, and ten days' journey brought them to the kingdom of Poh-nâ[5], where there are also more than three thousand monks, all students of the hînayâna. Proceeding from this place for three days, they again crossed the Indus, where the country on each side was low and level[6].

CHAPTER XV.

BHIDA. SYMPATHY OF MONKS WITH THE PILGRIMS.

AFTER they had crossed the river, there was a country named Pe-t'oo[7], where Buddhism was very flourishing, and (the monks) studied both the mahâyâna and hînayâna. When they saw their fellow-disciples from Ts'in passing along, they were moved with great pity and sympathy, and expressed themselves thus: 'How is it that these men

---

[1] All the texts have Hwuy-king. See note 2, page 36.

[2] A very natural exclamation, but out of place and inconsistent from the lips of Fâ-hien. The Chinese character 命, which he employed, may be rendered rightly by 'fate' or 'destiny;' but the fate is not unintelligent. The term implies a factor, or fa-tor, and supposes the ordination of Heaven or God. A Confucian idea for the moment overcame his Buddhism.

[3] Lo-e, or Rohî, is a name for Afghanistan; but only a portion of it can be here intended.

[4] We are now therefore in 404.

[5] No doubt the present district of Bannu, in the Lieutenant-Governorship of the Punjâb, between 32° 10′ and 33° 15′ N. lat., and 70° 26′ and 72° E. lon. See Hunter's Gazetteer of India, i, p. 393.

[6] They had then crossed the Indus before. They had done so, indeed, twice: first, from north to south, at Skardo or east of it; and second, as described in chap. vii.

[7] Bhida. Eitel says, 'The present Punjâb;' i.e. it was a portion of that.

from a border-land should have learned to become monks [1], and come for the sake of our doctrines from such a distance in search of the Law of Buddha?' They supplied them with what they needed, and treated them in accordance with the rules of the Law.

CHAPTER XVI.

ON TO MATHURÂ OR MUTTRA. CONDITION AND CUSTOMS OF CENTRAL INDIA; OF THE MONKS, VIHÂRAS, AND MONASTERIES.

FROM this place they travelled south-east, passing by a succession of very many monasteries, with a multitude of monks, who might be counted by myriads. After passing all these places, they came to a country named Ma-t'âou-lo [2]. They still followed the course of the P'oo-na [3] river, on the banks of which, left and right, there were twenty monasteries, which might contain three thousand monks; and (here) the Law of Buddha was still more flourishing. Everywhere, from the Sandy Desert, in all the countries of India, the kings had been firm believers in that Law. When they make their offerings to a community of monks, they take off their royal caps, and along with their relatives and ministers, supply them with food with their own hands. That done, (the king) has a carpet spread for himself on the ground, and sits down on it in front of the chairman;—they dare not presume to sit on couches in front of the community. The laws and ways, according to which the kings presented their offerings when Buddha was in the world, have been handed down to the present day.

All south from this is named the Middle Kingdom [4]. In it the cold and heat are finely tempered, and there is neither hoarfrost nor snow. The people are numerous and happy; they have not to register their households, or attend to any magistrates and their rules; only those who

---

[1] 'To come forth from their families;' that is, to become celibates, and adopt the tonsure.

[2] Muttra, 'the peacock city;' lat. 27° 30′ N., lon. 77° 43′ E. (Hunter); the birth-place of Kṛishṇa, whose emblem is the peacock.

[3] This must be the Jumna, or Yamunâ. Why it is called, as here, the P'oo-na has yet to be explained.

[4] In Pâli, Majjhima-desa, 'the Middle Country.' See Davids' 'Buddhist Birth Stories,' page 61, note.

cultivate the royal land have to pay (a portion of) the gain from it. If they want to go, they go; if they want to stay on, they stay. The king governs without decapitation or (other) corporal punishments. Criminals are simply fined, lightly or heavily, according to the circumstances (of each case). Even in cases of repeated attempts at wicked rebellion, they only have their right hands cut off. The king's body-guards and attendants all have salaries. Throughout the whole country the people do not kill any living creature, nor drink intoxicating liquor, nor eat onions or garlic. The only exception is that of the Chaṇḍâlas[1]. That is the name for those who are (held to be) wicked men, and live apart from others. When they enter the gate of a city or a market-place, they strike a piece of wood to make themselves known, so that men know and avoid them, and do not come into contact with them. In that country they do not keep pigs and fowls, and do not sell live cattle; in the markets there are no butchers' shops and no dealers in intoxicating drink. In buying and selling commodities they use cowries[2]. Only the Chaṇḍâlas are fishermen and hunters, and sell flesh meat.

After Buddha attained to pari-nirvâṇa[3] the kings of the various countries and the heads of the Vaiśyas[4] built vihâras for the priests, and endowed them with fields, houses, gardens, and orchards, along with the resident populations and their cattle, the grants being engraved on plates of metal[5], so that afterwards they were handed down from king to king, without any one daring to annul them, and they remain even to the present time.

---

[1] Eitel (pp. 145, 6) says, 'The name Chaṇḍâlas is explained by "butchers," "wicked men," and those who carry "the awful flag," to warn off their betters;—the lowest and most despised caste of India, members of which, however, when converted, were admitted even into the ranks of the priesthood.'

[2] 'Cowries;' 貝齒, not 'shells and ivory,' as one might suppose; but cowries alone, the second term entering into the name from the marks inside the edge of the shell, resembling 'the teeth of fishes.'

[3] See note 3, page 33, Buddha's pari-nirvâṇa is equivalent to Buddha's death.

[4] See note 1, page 38. The order of the characters is different here, but with the same meaning.

[5] See the preparation of such a deed of grant in a special case, as related in chap. xxxix. No doubt in Fâ-hien's time, and long before and after it, it was the custom to engrave such deeds on plates of metal.

The regular business of the monks is to perform acts of meritorious virtue, and to recite their Sûtras and sit wrapt in meditation. When stranger monks arrive (at any monastery), the old residents meet and receive them, carry for them their clothes and alms-bowl, give them water to wash their feet, oil with which to anoint them, and the liquid food permitted out of the regular hours[1]. When (the stranger) has enjoyed a very brief rest, they further ask the number of years that he has been a monk, after which he receives a sleeping apartment with its appurtenances, according to his regular order, and everything is done for him which the rules prescribe[2].

Where a community of monks resides, they erect topes to Śâriputtra[3], to Mahâ-maudgalyâyana[4], and to Ânanda[5], and also topes (in honour) of

---

[1] 'No monk can eat solid food except between sunrise and noon,' and total abstinence from intoxicating drinks is obligatory (Davids' Manual, p. 163). Food eaten at any other part of the day is called vikâla, and forbidden; but a weary traveller might receive unseasonable refreshment, consisting, as Watters has shown (Ch. Rev. viii. 282), of honey, butter, treacle, and sesamum oil.

[2] The expression here is somewhat perplexing; but it occurs again in chap. xxxviii; and the meaning is clear. See Watters, Ch. Rev. viii. 282, 3. The rules are given at length in the Sacred Books of the East, vol. xx, p. 272 and foll., and p. 279 and foll.

[3] Śâriputtra (Singh. Seriyut) was one of the principal disciples of Buddha, and indeed the most learned and ingenious of them all, so that he obtained the title of 智慧, 'knowledge and wisdom.' He is also called Buddha's 'right-hand attendant.' His name is derived from that of his mother Śârikâ, the wife of Tishya, a native of Nalanda. In Spence Hardy, he often appears under the name of Upatissa (Upa-tishya), derived from his father. Several Śâstras are ascribed to him, and indeed the followers of the Abhidharma look on him as their founder. He died before Śâkyamuni; but is to reappear as a future Buddha. Eitel, pp. 123, 124.

[4] Mugalan, the Singhalese name of this disciple, is more pronounceable. He also was one of the principal disciples, called Buddha's 'left-hand attendant.' He was distinguished for his power of vision, and his magic powers. The name in the text is derived from the former attribute, and it was by the latter that he took up an artist to Tushita to get a view of Śâkyamuni, and so make a statue of him. (Compare the similar story in chap. vi.) He went to hell, and released his mother. He also died before Śâkyamuni, and is to reappear as Buddha. Eitel, p. 65.

[5] See note 2, page 33.

the Abhidharma[1], the Vinaya[1], and the Sûtras[1]. A month after the (annual season of) rest, the families which are looking out for blessing stimulate one another[2] to make offerings to the monks, and send round to them the liquid food which may be taken out of the ordinary hours. All the monks come together in a great assembly, and preach the Law[3]; after which offerings are presented at the tope of Śâriputtra, with all kinds of flowers and incense. All through the night lamps are kept burning, and skilful musicians are employed to perform[4].

When Śâriputtra was a great Brahman, he went to Buddha, and begged (to be permitted) to quit his family (and become a monk). The great Mugalan and the great Kaśyapa[5] also did the same. The bhikshuṇîs[6] for the most part make their offerings at the tope of Ânanda, because it was he who requested the World-honoured one to allow females to quit their families (and become nuns). The Śrâmaṇeras[7] mostly

---

[1] The different parts of the tripiṭaka. See note 2, page 10.

[2] A passage rather difficult to construe. The 'families' would be those more devout than their neighbours.

[3] One rarely hears this preaching in China. It struck me most as I once heard it at Osaka in Japan. There was a pulpit in a large hall of the temple, and the audience sat around on the matted floor. One priest took the pulpit after another; and the hearers nodded their heads occasionally, and indicated their sympathy with a sentiment now and then by an audible 'h'm,' which reminded me of Carlyle's description of meetings of 'The Ironsides' of Cromwell.

[4] This last statement is wanting in the Chinese editions.

[5] There was a Kaśyapa Buddha, anterior to Śâkyamuni. But this Mahâkaśyapa was a Brahman of Magadha, who was converted by Buddha, and became one of his disciples. He took the lead after Śâkyamuni's death, convoked and directed the first synod, from which his title of Arya-sthavira is derived. As the first compiler of the Canon, he is considered the fountain of Chinese orthodoxy, and counted as the first patriarch. He also is to be reborn as a Buddha. Eitel, p. 64.

[6] The bhikshuṇîs are the female monks or nuns, subject to the same rules as the bhikshus, and also to special ordinances of restraint. See Hardy's E. M., chap. 17. See also Sacred Books of the East, vol. xx, p. 321.

[7] The Śrâmaṇeras are the novices, male or female, who have vowed to

make their offerings to Râhula[1]. The professors of the Abhidharma[2] make their offerings to it; those of the Vinaya[2] to it. Every year there is one such offering, and each class has its own day for it. Students of the mahâyâna present offerings to the Prajñâ-pâramitâ[3], to Mañjuśrî[4], and to Kwan-she-yin[5]. When the monks have done receiving their

---

observe the Shikshâpada, or ten commandments. Fâ-hien was himself one of them from his childhood. Having heard the Trîsharaṇa, or threefold formula of Refuge,—'I take refuge in Buddha; the Law; the Church,—the novice undertakes to observe the ten precepts that forbid—(1) destroying life; (2) stealing; (3) impurity; (4) lying; (5) intoxicating drinks; (6) eating after midday; (7) dancing, singing, music, and stage-plays; (8) garlands, scents, unguents, and ornaments; (9) high or broad couches; (10) receiving gold or silver.' Davids' Manual, p. 160; Hardy's E. M., pp. 23, 24.

[1] The eldest son of Śâkyamuni by Yaśodharâ. Converted to Buddhism, he followed his father as an attendant; and after Buddha's death became the founder of a philosophical realistic school (vaibhâshika). He is now revered as the patron saint of all novices, and is to be reborn as the eldest son of every future Buddha. Eitel, p. 101. His mother also is to be reborn as Buddha.

[2] Note 1, page 45.

[3] There are six (sometimes increased to ten) pâramitâs, 'means of passing to nirvâṇa:—Charity; morality; patience; energy; tranquil contemplation; wisdom (prajñâ); made up to ten by use of the proper means; science; pious vows; and force of purpose. But it is only prajñâ which carries men across the saṃsâra to the shores of nirvâṇa.' Eitel, p. 90.

[4] According to Eitel (pp. 71, 72), 'A famous Bodhisattva, now specially worshipped in Shan-se, whose antecedents are a hopeless jumble of history and fable. Fâ-hien found him here worshipped by followers of the mahâyâna school; but Hsüan-chwang connects his worship with the yogachara or tantra-magic school. The mahâyâna school regard him as the apotheosis of perfect wisdom. His most common titles are Mahâmati, "Great wisdom," and Kumâra-râja, "King of teaching, with a thousand arms and a hundred alms-bowls."'

[5] Kwan-she-yin and the dogmas about him or her are as great a mystery as Mañjuśrî. The Chinese name is a mistranslation of the Sanskrit name Avalokiteśvara, 'On-looking Sovereign,' or even 'On-looking Self-Existent,' and means 'Regarding or Looking on the sounds of the world,'='Hearer of Prayer.' Originally, and still in Thibet, Avalokiteśvara had only male attributes,

annual tribute (from the harvests)[1], the Heads of the Vaiśyas and all the Brahmans bring clothes and such other articles as the monks require for use, and distribute among them. The monks, having received them, also proceed to give portions to one another. From the nirvâṇa of Buddha[2], the forms of ceremony, laws, and rules, practised by the sacred communities, have been handed down from one generation to another without interruption.

From the place where (the travellers) crossed the Indus to South India, and on to the Southern Sea, a distance of forty or fifty thousand le, all is level plain. There are no large hills with streams (among them); there are simply the waters of the rivers.

CHAPTER XVII.

SAṄKÂŚYA. BUDDHA'S ASCENT TO AND DESCENT FROM THE TRAYASTRIṂŚAS HEAVEN, AND OTHER LEGENDS.

FROM this they proceeded south-east for eighteen yojanas, and found themselves in a kingdom called Saṅkâśya[3], at the place where Buddha came

---

but in China and Japan (Kwannon), this deity (such popularly she is) is represented as a woman, 'Kwan-yin, the greatly gentle, with a thousand arms and a thousand eyes;' and has her principal seat in the island of P'oo-t'oo, on the China coast, which is a regular place of pilgrimage. To the worshippers of whom Fâ-hien speaks, Kwan-she-yin would only be Avalokiteśvara. How he was converted into the 'goddess of mercy,' and her worship took the place which it now has in China, is a difficult inquiry, which would take much time and space, and not be brought after all, so far as I see, to a satisfactory conclusion. See Eitel's Handbook, pp. 18–20, and his Three Lectures on Buddhism (third edition), pp. 124–131. I was talking on the subject once with an intelligent Chinese gentleman, when he remarked, 'Have you not much the same thing in Europe in the worship of Mary?'

[1] Compare what is said in chap. v.

[2] This nirvâṇa of Buddha must be—not his death, but his attaining to Buddhaship.

[3] The name is still remaining in Samkassam, a village forty-five miles north-west of Canouge, lat. 27° 3′ N., lon. 79° 50′ E.

down, after ascending to the Trayastriṃśas heaven[1], and there preaching for three months his Law for the benefit of his mother[2]. Buddha had gone up to this heaven by his supernatural power[3], without letting his disciples know; but seven days before the completion (of the three months) he laid aside his invisibility[3], and Anuruddha[4], with his heavenly eyes[4], saw the World-honoured one, and immediately said to the honoured one, the great Mugalan, 'Do you go and salute the World-honoured one.' Mugalan forthwith went, and with head and face did homage at (Buddha's) feet. They then saluted and questioned each other, and when this was over, Buddha said to Mugalan, 'Seven days after this I will go down to Jambudvîpa;' and thereupon Mugalan returned. At this time the great kings of eight countries with their ministers and people, not having seen Buddha for a long time, were all thirstily looking up for him, and had collected in clouds in this kingdom to wait for the World-honoured one.

---

[1] The heaven of Indra or Śâkya, meaning 'the heaven of thirty-three classes,' a name which has been explained both historically and mythologically. 'The description of it,' says Eitel, p. 148, 'tallies in all respects with the Svarga of Brahmanic mythology. It is situated between the four peaks of the Meru, and consists of thirty-two cities of devas, eight on each of the four corners of the mountain. Indra's capital of Bellevue is in the centre. There he is enthroned, with a thousand heads and a thousand eyes, and four arms grasping the vajra, with his wife and 119,000 concubines. There he receives the monthly reports of the four Mahârâjas, concerning the progress of good and evil in the world,' &c. &c.

[2] Buddha's mother, Mâyâ and Mahâmâyâ, the mater immaculata of the Buddhists, died seven days after his birth. Eitel says, 'Reborn in Tushita, she was visited there by her son and converted.' The Tushita heaven was a more likely place to find her in than the Trayastriṃśas; but was the former a part of the latter? Hardy gives a long account of Buddha's visit to the Trayastriṃśas (M. B., pp. 298–302), which he calls Tawutisâ, and speaks of his mother (Mâtru) in it, who had now become a deva by the changing of her sex.

[3] Compare the account of the Arhat's conveyance of the artist to the Tushita heaven in chap. v. The first expression here is more comprehensive.

[4] Anuruddha was a first cousin of Śâkyamuni, being the son of his uncle Amṛitodana. He is often mentioned in the account we have of Buddha's last moments. His special gift was the divyachakshus or 'heavenly eye,' the first of the six abhijñâs or 'supernatural talents,' the faculty of comprehending in one

Then the bhikshuṇî Utpala[1] thought in her heart, 'To-day the kings, with their ministers and people, will all be meeting (and welcoming) Buddha. I am (but) a woman; how shall I succeed in being the first to see him[2]?' Buddha immediately, by his spirit-like power, changed her into the appearance of a holy Chakravartti[3] king, and she was the foremost of all in doing reverence to him.

As Buddha descended from his position aloft in the Trayastriṃśas heaven, when he was coming down, there were made to appear three flights of precious steps. Buddha was on the middle flight, the steps of which were composed of the seven precious substances. The king of Brahma-loka[4] also made a flight of silver steps appear on the right side, (where he was seen) attending with a white chowry in his hand. Śakra,

---

instantaneous view, or by intuition, all beings in all worlds. 'He could see,' says Hardy, M. B., p. 232, 'all things in 100,000 sakvalas as plainly as a mustard seed held in the hand.'

[1] Eitel gives the name Utpala with the same Chinese phonetisation as in the text, but not as the name of any bhikshuṇî. The Sanskrit word, however, is explained by 'blue lotus flowers;' and Hsüan-chwang calls her the nun 'Lotus-flower colour (蓮花色);'—the same as Hardy's Upulwan and Uppalawarnâ.

[2] Perhaps we should read here 'to see Buddha,' and then ascribe the transformation to the nun herself. It depends on the punctuation which view we adopt; and in the structure of the passage, there is nothing to indicate that the stop should be made before or after 'Buddha.' And the one view is as reasonable, or rather as unreasonable, as the other.

[3] 'A holy king who turns the wheel;' that is, the military conqueror and monarch of the whole or part of a universe. 'The symbol,' says Eitel (p. 142), 'of such a king is the chakra or wheel, for when he ascends the throne, a chakra falls from heaven, indicating by its material (gold, silver, copper, or iron) the extent and character of his reign. The office, however, of the highest Chakravartti, who hurls his wheel among his enemies, is inferior to the peaceful mission of a Buddha, who meekly turns the wheel of the Law, and conquers every universe by his teaching.'

[4] This was Brahma, the first person of the Brahmanical Trimurti, adopted by Buddhism, but placed in an inferior position, and surpassed by every Buddhist saint who attains to bodhi.

Ruler of Devas[1], made (a flight of) steps of purple gold on the left side, (where he was seen) attending and holding an umbrella of the seven precious substances. An innumerable multitude of the devas[2] followed Buddha in his descent. When he was come down, the three flights all disappeared in the ground, excepting seven steps, which continued to be visible. Afterwards king Aśoka, wishing to know where their ends rested, sent men to dig and see. They went down to the yellow springs[3] without reaching the bottom of the steps, and from this the king received an increase to his reverence and faith, and built a vihâra over the steps, with a standing image, sixteen cubits in height, right over the middle flight. Behind the vihâra he erected a stone pillar, about fifty cubits high[4], with a lion on the top of it[5]. Let into the pillar, on each of its four sides[6], there is an image of Buddha, inside and out[7] shining and transparent, and pure as it were of lapis lazuli. Some teachers of another doctrine[8] once disputed with the Śramaṇas about (the right to) this as a place of residence, and the latter were having the worst of

---

[1] See note 2, p. 30.

[2] See note 3, p. 19.

[3] A common name for the earth below, where, on digging, water is found.

[4] The height is given as thirty chow, the chow being the distance from the elbow to the finger-tip, which is variously estimated.

[5] A note of Mr. Beal says on this:—'General Cunningham, who visited the spot (1862), found a pillar, evidently of the age of Aśoka, with a well-carved elephant on the top, which, however, was minus trunk and tail. He supposes this to be the pillar seen by Fâ-hien, who mistook the top of it for a lion. It is possible such a mistake may have been made, as in the account of one of the pillars at Śrâvastî, Fâ-hien says an ox formed the capital, whilst Hsüan-chwang calls it an elephant (p. 19, Arch. Survey).'

[6] That is, in niches on the sides. The pillar or column must have been square.

[7] Equivalent to 'all through.'

[8] Has always been translated 'heretical teachers;' but I eschew the terms heresy and heretical. The parties would not be Buddhists of any creed or school, but Brahmans or of some other false doctrine, as Fâ-hien deemed it. The Chinese term means 'outside' or 'foreign;'—in Pâli, aññа-titthiyâ,='those belonging to another school.'

the argument, when they took an oath on both sides on the condition that, if the place did indeed belong to the Śramaṇas, there should be some marvellous attestation of it. When these words had been spoken, the lion on the top gave a great roar, thus giving the proof; on which their opponents were frightened, bowed to the decision, and withdrew.

Through Buddha having for three months partaken of the food of heaven, his body emitted a heavenly fragrance, unlike that of an ordinary man. He went immediately and bathed; and afterwards, at the spot where he did so, a bathing-house was built, which is still existing. At the place where the bhikshuṇî Utpala was the first to do reverence to Buddha, a tope has now been built.

At the places where Buddha, when he was in the world, cut his hair and nails[1], topes are erected; and where the three Buddhas[2] that preceded Śâkyamuni Buddha and he himself sat; where they walked[3], and where images of their persons were made. At all these places topes were made, and are still existing. At the place where Śakra, Ruler of the Devas, and the king of the Brahma-loka followed Buddha down (from the Trayastriṃśas heaven) they have also raised a tope.

At this place the monks and nuns may be a thousand, who all receive

---

[1] See above, p. 39.

[2] These three predecessors of Śâkyamuni were the three Buddhas of the present or Mahâ-bhadra Kalpa, of which he was the fourth, and Maitreya is to be the fifth and last. They were: (1) Krakuchanda (Pâli, Kakusanda), 'he who readily solves all doubts;' a scion of the Kaśyapa family. Human life reached in his time 40,000 years, and so many persons were converted by him. (2) Kanakamuni (Pâli, Konâgamana), 'body radiant with the colour of pure gold;' of the same family. Human life reached in his time 30,000 years, and so many persons were converted by him. (3) Kâśyapa (Pâli, Kassapa), 'swallower of light.' Human life reached in his time 20,000 years, and so many persons were converted by him. See Eitel, under the several names; Hardy's M. B., pp. 95–97; and Davids' 'Buddhist Birth Stories,' p. 51.

[3] That is, walked in meditation. Such places are called Chaṅkramaṇa (Pâli, Chankama); promenades or corridors connected with a monastery, made sometimes with costly stones, for the purpose of peripatetic meditation. The 'sitting' would be not because of weariness or for rest, but for meditation. E. H., p. 144.

their food from the common store, and pursue their studies, some of the mahâyâna and some of the hînayâna. Where they live, there is a white-eared dragon, which acts the part of dânapati[1] to the community of these monks, causing abundant harvests in the country, and the enriching rains to come in season, without the occurrence of any calamities, so that the monks enjoy their repose and ease. In gratitude for its kindness, they have made for it a dragon-house, with a carpet for it to sit on, and appointed for it a diet of blessing, which they present for its nourishment. Every day they set apart three of their number to go to its house, and eat there. Whenever the summer retreat is ended, the dragon straightway changes its form, and appears as a small snake[2], with white spots at the side of its ears. As soon as the monks recognise it, they fill a copper vessel with cream, into which they put the creature, and then carry it round from the one who has the highest seat (at their tables) to him who has the lowest, when it appears as if saluting them. When it has been taken round, immediately it disappears; and every year it thus comes forth once. The country is very productive, and the people are prosperous, and happy beyond comparison. When people of other countries come to it, they are exceedingly attentive to them all, and supply them with what they need.

Fifty yojanas north-west from the monastery there is another, called 'The Great Heap[3].' Great Heap was the name of a wicked demon, who was converted by Buddha, and men subsequently at this place reared a vihâra. When it was being made over to an Arhat by pouring water on his hands[4], some drops fell on the ground. They are still on

---

[1] See note 2, p. 11.

[2] The character in my Corean copy is 蜡, which must be a mistake for the 蛇 of the Chinese editions. Otherwise, the meaning would be 'a small medusa.'

[3] The reading here seems to me a great improvement on that of the Chinese editions, which means 'Fire Limit.' Buddha, it is said, 本 converted this demon, which Chinese character Beal rendered at first by 'in one of his incarnations;' and in his revised version he has 'himself.' The difference between Fâ-hien's usage of 本 and 昔 throughout his narrative is quite marked. 本 always refers to the doings of Śâkyamuni; 昔, 'formerly,' is often used of him and others in the sense of 'in a former age or birth.'

[4] See Hardy, M. B., p. 194:—'As a token of the giving over of the garden,

the spot, and however they may be brushed away and removed, they continue to be visible, and cannot be made to disappear.

At this place there is also a tope to Buddha, where a good spirit constantly keeps (all about it) swept and watered, without any labour of man being required. A king of corrupt views once said, 'Since you are able to do this, I will lead a multitude of troops and reside there till the dirt and filth has increased and accumulated, and (see) whether you can cleanse it away or not.' The spirit thereupon raised a great wind, which blew (the filth away), and made the place pure.

At this place there are a hundred small topes, at which a man may keep counting a whole day without being able to know (their exact number). If he be firmly bent on knowing it, he will place a man by the side of each tope. When this is done, proceeding to count the number of the men, whether they be many or few, he will not get to know (the number)[1].

There is a monastery, containing perhaps 600 or 700 monks, in which there is a place where a Pratyeka Buddha[2] used to take his food. The nirvâṇa ground (where he was burned[3] after death) is as large as a carriage wheel; and while grass grows all around, on this spot there is none. The ground also where he dried his clothes produces no grass, but the impression of them, where they lay on it, continues to the present day.

CHAPTER XVIII.

KANYÂKUBJA, OR CANOUGE. BUDDHA'S PREACHING.

FÂ-HIEN stayed at the Dragon vihâra till after the summer retreat[4], and then, travelling to the south-east for seven yojanas, he arrived at the

---

the king poured water upon the hands of Buddha; and from this time it became one of the principal residences of the sage.'

[1] This would seem to be absurd; but the writer evidently intended to convey the idea that there was something mysterious about the number of the topes.

[2] See note 2, p. 40.

[3] This seems to be the meaning. The bodies of the monks are all burned. Hardy's E. M., pp. 322–324.

[4] We are now, probably, in 405.

city of Kanyâkubja[1], lying along the Ganges[2]. There are two monasteries in it, the inmates of which are students of the hînayâna. At a distance from the city of six or seven le, on the west, on the northern bank of the Ganges, is a place where Buddha preached the Law to his disciples. It has been handed down that his subjects of discourse were such as 'The bitterness and vanity (of life) as impermanent and uncertain,' and that 'The body is as a bubble or foam on the water.' At this spot a tope was erected, and still exists.

Having crossed the Ganges, and gone south for three yojanas, (the travellers) arrived at a village named Â-le[3], containing places where Buddha preached the Law, where he sat, and where he walked, at all of which topes have been built.

CHAPTER XIX.

SHÂ-CHE. LEGEND OF BUDDHA'S DANTA-KÂSHṬHA.

GOING on from this to the south-east for three yojanas, they came to the great kingdom of Shâ-che[4]. As you go out of the city of Shâ-che by the southern gate, on the east of the road (is the place) where Buddha, after he had chewed his willow branch[5], stuck it in the ground, when it

---

[1] Canouge, the latitude and longitude of which have been given in a previous note. The Sanskrit name means 'the city of humpbacked maidens;' with reference to the legend of the hundred daughters of king Brahma-datta, who were made deformed by the curse of the ṛishi Mahâ-vṛiksha, whose overtures they had refused. E. H., p. 51.

[2] Gaṅgâ, explained by 'Blessed water,' and 'Come from heaven to earth.'

[3] This village (the Chinese editions read 'forest') has hardly been clearly identified.

[4] Shâ-che should probably be Shâ-khe, making Cunningham's identification of the name with the present Saket still more likely. The change of 祗 into 祇 is slight; and, indeed, the Khang-hsî dictionary thinks the two characters should be but one and the same.

[5] This was, no doubt, what was called the danta-kâshṭha, or 'dental wood,' mostly a bit of the ficus Indicus or banyan tree, which the monk chews every morning to cleanse his teeth, and for the purpose of health generally. The

forthwith grew up seven cubits, (at which height it remained) neither increasing nor diminishing. The Brahmans with their contrary doctrines[1] became angry and jealous. Sometimes they cut the tree down, sometimes they plucked it up, and cast it to a distance, but it grew again on the same spot as at first. Here also is the place where the four Buddhas walked and sat, and at which a tope was built that is still existing.

CHAPTER XX.

KOŚALA AND ŚRÂVASTÎ. THE JETAVANA VIHÂRA AND OTHER MEMORIALS AND LEGENDS OF BUDDHA. SYMPATHY OF THE MONKS WITH THE PILGRIMS.

GOING on from this to the south, for eight yojanas, (the travellers) came to the city of Śrâvastî[2] in the kingdom of Kośala[3], in which the inhabitants were few and far between, amounting in all (only) to a few more than two hundred families; the city where king Prasenajit[4] ruled, and the place of the old vihâra of Mahâ-prajâpatî[5]; of the well and walls of

---

Chinese, not having the banyan, have used, or at least Fâ-hien used, Yang (楊, the general name for the willow) instead of it.

[1] Are two classes of opponents, or only one, intended here, so that we should read 'all the unbelievers and Brahmans,' or 'heretics and Brahmans?' I think the Brahmans were also 'the unbelievers' and 'heretics,' having 外道, views and ways outside of, and opposed to, Buddha's.

[2] In Singhalese, Sewet; here evidently the capital of Kośala. It is placed by Cunningham (Archæological Survey) on the south bank of the Rapti, about fifty-eight miles north of Ayodyâ or Oude. There are still the ruins of a great town, the name being Sâhet Mâhat. It was in this town, or in its neighbourhood, that Śâkyamuni spent many years of his life after he became Buddha.

[3] There were two Indian kingdoms of this name, a southern and northern. This was the northern, a part of the present Oudh.

[4] In Singhalese, Pase-naḍi, meaning 'leader of the victorious army.' He was one of the earliest converts and chief patrons of Śâkyamuni. Eitel calls him (p. 95) one of the originators of Buddhist idolatry, because of the statue which is mentioned in this chapter. See Hardy's M. B., pp. 283, 284, et al.

[5] Explained by 'Path of Love,' and 'Lord of Life.' Prajâpatî was aunt and

(the house of) the (Vaiśya) head Sudatta[1]; and where the Aṅgulimâlya[2] became an Arhat, and his body was (afterwards) burned on his attaining to pari-nirvâṇa. At all these places topes were subsequently erected, which are still existing in the city. The Brahmans, with their contrary doctrine, became full of hatred and envy in their hearts, and wished to destroy them, but there came from the heavens such a storm of crashing thunder and flashing lightning that they were not able in the end to effect their purpose.

As you go out from the city by the south gate, and 1,200 paces from it, the (Vaiśya) head Sudatta built a vihâra, facing the south; and when the door was open, on each side of it there was a stone pillar, with the figure of a wheel on the top of that on the left, and the figure of an ox on the top of that on the right. On the left and right of the building the ponds of water clear and pure, the thickets of trees always luxuriant, and the numerous flowers of various hues, constituted a lovely scene, the whole forming what is called the Jetavana vihâra[3].

When Buddha went up to the Trayastriṃśas heaven[4], and preached the Law for the benefit of his mother[4], (after he had been absent for)

---

nurse of Śâkyamuni, the first woman admitted to the monkhood, and the first superior of the first Buddhistic convent. She is yet to become a Buddha.

[1] Sudatta, meaning 'almsgiver,' was the original name of Anâtha-piṇḍika (or Piṇḍada), a wealthy householder, or Vaiśya head, of Śrâvastî, famous for his liberality (Hardy, Anepidu). Of his old house, only the well and walls remained at the time of Fâ-hien's visit to Śrâvastî.

[2] The Aṅgulimâlya were a sect or set of Śivaitic fanatics, who made assassination a religious act. The one of them here mentioned had joined them by the force of circumstances. Being converted by Buddha, he became a monk; but when it is said in the text that he 'got the Tâo,' or doctrine, I think that expression implies more than his conversion, and is equivalent to his becoming an Arhat. His name in Pâli is Aṅgulimâla. That he did become an Arhat is clear from his autobiographical poem in the 'Songs of the Theras.'

[3] Eitel (p. 37) says:—'A noted vihâra in the suburbs of Śrâvastî, erected in a park which Anâtha-piṇḍika bought of prince Jeta, the son of Prasenajit. Śâkyamuni made this place his favourite residence for many years. Most of the Sûtras (authentic and supposititious) date from this spot.'

[4] See chapter xvii.

ninety days, Prasenajit, longing to see him, caused an image of him to be carved in Gośîrsha Chandana wood[1], and put in the place where he usually sat. When Buddha on his return entered the vihâra, this image immediately left its place, and came forth to meet him. Buddha said to it, 'Return to your seat. After I have attained to pari-nirvâṇa, you will serve as a pattern to the four classes of my disciples[2],' and on this the image returned to its seat. This was the very first of all the images (of Buddha), and that which men subsequently copied. Buddha then removed, and dwelt in a small vihâra on the south side (of the other), a different place from that containing the image, and twenty paces distant from it.

The Jetavana vihâra was originally of seven storeys. The kings and people of the countries around vied with one another in their offerings, hanging up about it silken streamers and canopies, scattering flowers, burning incense, and lighting lamps, so as to make the night as bright as the day. This they did day after day without ceasing. (It happened that) a rat, carrying in its mouth the wick of a lamp, set one of the streamers or canopies on fire, which caught the vihâra, and the seven storeys were all consumed. The kings, with their officers and people, were all very sad and distressed, supposing that the sandal-wood image had been burned; but lo! after four or five days, when the door of a small vihâra on the east was opened, there was immediately seen the original image. They were all greatly rejoiced, and co-operated in restoring the vihâra. When they had succeeded in completing two storeys, they removed the image back to its former place.

When Fâ-hien and Tâo-ching first arrived at the Jetavana monastery, and thought how the World-honoured one had formerly resided

---

[1] See chapter xiii.

[2] Ârya, meaning 'honourable,' 'venerable,' is a title given only to those who have mastered the four spiritual truths:—(1) that 'misery' is a necessary condition of all sentient existence; this is duḥkha: (2) that the 'accumulation' of misery is caused by the passions; this is samudaya: (3) that the 'extinction' of passion is possible; this is nirodha: and (4) that the 'path' leads to the extinction of passion; which is mârga. According to their attainment of these truths, the Âryas, or followers of Buddha, are distinguished into four classes,—Śrotâpannas, Sakṛidâgâmins, Anâgâmins, and Ârhats. E. H., p. 14.

there for twenty-five years, painful reflections arose in their minds. Born in a border-land, along with their like-minded friends, they had travelled through so many kingdoms; some of those friends had returned (to their own land), and some had (died), proving the impermanence and uncertainty of life; and to-day they saw the place where Buddha had lived now unoccupied by him. They were melancholy through their pain of heart, and the crowd of monks came out, and asked them from what kingdom they were come. 'We are come,' they replied, 'from the land of Han.' 'Strange,' said the monks with a sigh, 'that men of a border country should be able to come here in search of our Law!' Then they said to one another, 'During all the time that we, preceptors and monks[1], have succeeded to one another, we have never seen men of Han, followers of our system, arrive here.'

Four le to the north-west of the vihâra there is a grove called 'The Getting of Eyes.' Formerly there were five hundred blind men, who lived here in order that they might be near the vihâra[2]. Buddha

---

[1] This is the first time that Fâ-hien employs the name Ho-shang (和尙), which is now popularly used in China for all Buddhist monks without distinction of rank or office. It is the representative of the Sanskrit term Upadhyâya, 'explained,' says Eitel (p. 155), by 'a self-taught teacher,' or by 'he who knows what is sinful and what is not sinful,' with the note, 'In India the vernacular of this term is 磒社 (? munshee [? Bonze]); in Kustana and Kashgar they say 鶻社 (hwa-shay); and from the latter term are derived the Chinese synonyms, 和闍 (ho-shay) and 和尙 (ho-shang).' The Indian term was originally a designation for those who teach only a part of the Vedas, the Vedâṅgas. Adopted by Buddhists of Central Asia, it was made to signify the priests of the older ritual, in distinction from the Lamas. In China it has been used first as a synonym for 法師, monks engaged in popular teaching (teachers of the Law), in distinction from 律師, disciplinists, and 禪師, contemplative philosophers (meditationists); then it was used to designate the abbots of monasteries. But it is now popularly applied to all Buddhist monks. In the text there seems to be implied some distinction between the 'teachers' and the 'ho-shang;'—probably, the Pâli Â*k*ariya and Upa*ggh*âya; see Sacred Books of the East, vol. xiii, Vinaya Texts, pp. 178, 179.

[2] It might be added, 'as depending on it,' in order to bring out the full meaning of the 依 in the text. If I recollect aright, the help of the police

preached his Law to them, and they all got back their eyesight. Full of joy, they stuck their staves in the earth, and with their heads and faces on the ground, did reverence. The staves immediately began to grow, and they grew to be great. People made much of them, and no one dared to cut them down, so that they came to form a grove. It was in this way that it got its name, and most of the Jetavana monks, after they had taken their midday meal, went to the grove, and sat there in meditation.

Six or seven le north-east from the Jetavana, mother Vaiśakha[1] built another vihâra, to which she invited Buddha and his monks, and which is still existing.

To each of the great residences for the monks at the Jetavana vihâra there were two gates, one facing the east and the other facing the north. The park (containing the whole) was the space of ground which the (Vaiśya) head Sudatta purchased by covering it with gold coins. The vihâra was exactly in the centre. Here Buddha lived for a longer time than at any other place, preaching his Law and converting men. At the places where he walked and sat they also (subsequently) reared topes, each having its particular name; and here was the place where Sundari[2] murdered a person and then falsely charged Buddha (with the crime). Outside the east gate of the Jetavana, at a distance of seventy paces to the north, on the west of the road, Buddha held a discussion

---

had to be called in at Hongkong in its early years, to keep the approaches to the Cathedral free from the number of beggars, who squatted down there during service, hoping that the hearers would come out with softened hearts, and disposed to be charitable. I found the popular tutelary temples in Peking and other places, and the path up Mount T'âi in Shan-lung similarly frequented.

[1] The wife of Anâtha-piṇḍika in note 1, p. 56, and who became 'mother-superior' of many nunneries. See her history in M. B., pp. 220–227. I am surprised it does not end with the statement that she is to become a Buddha.

[2] See E. H., p. 136. Hsüan-chwang does not give the name of this murderer; see in Julien's 'Vie et Voyages de Hiouen-thsang,' p. 125,—'a heretical Brahman killed a woman and calumniated Buddha.' See also the fuller account in Beal's 'Records of Western Countries,' pp. 7, 8, where the murder is committed by several Brahmachârins. In this passage Beal makes Sundari to be the name of the murdered person (a harlot). But the text cannot be so construed.

with the (advocates of the) ninety-six schemes of erroneous doctrine, when the king and his great officers, the householders, and people were all assembled in crowds to hear it. Then a woman belonging to one of the erroneous systems, by name Chañchamana [1], prompted by the envious hatred in her heart, and having put on (extra) clothes in front of her person, so as to give her the appearance of being with child, falsely accused Buddha before all the assembly of having acted unlawfully (towards her). On this, Śakra, Ruler of Devas, changed himself and some devas into white mice, which bit through the strings about her waist; and when this was done, the (extra) clothes which she wore dropt down on the ground. The earth at the same time was rent, and she went (down) alive into hell [2]. (This) also is the place where Devadatta [3], trying with empoisoned claws to injure Buddha, went down alive into hell. Men subsequently set up marks to distinguish where both these events took place.

Further, at the place where the discussion took place, they reared a vihâra rather more than sixty cubits high, having in it an image of Buddha in a sitting posture. On the east of the road there was a devâlaya [4] of (one of) the contrary systems, called 'The Shadow Covered,'

---

[1] Eitel (p. 144) calls her Chañcha; in Singhalese, Chinchi. See the story about her, M. B., pp. 275–277.

[2] 'Earth's prison,' or 'one of Earth's prisons.' It was the Avîchi nâraka to which she went, the last of the eight hot prisons, where the culprits die, and are born again in uninterrupted succession (such being the meaning of Avîchi), though not without hope of final redemption. E. H., p. 21.

[3] Devadatta was brother of Ânanda, and a near relative therefore of Śâkyamuni. He was the deadly enemy, however, of the latter. He had become so in an earlier state of existence, and the hatred continued in every successive birth, through which they reappeared in the world. See the accounts of him, and of his various devices against Buddha, and his own destruction at the last, in M. B., pp. 315–321, 326–330; and still better, in the Sacred Books of the East, vol. xx, Vinaya Texts, pp. 233–265. For the particular attempt referred to in the text, see 'The Life of the Buddha,' p. 107. When he was engulphed, and the flames were around him, he cried out to Buddha to save him, and we are told that he is expected yet to appear as a Buddha under the name of Devarâja, in a universe called Deva-soppana. E. H., p. 39.

[4] 'A devâlaya (天寺 or 天祠), a place in which a deva is worshipped,

right opposite the vihâra on the place of discussion, with (only) the road between them, and also rather more than sixty cubits high. The reason why it was called 'The Shadow Covered' was this:—When the sun was in the west, the shadow of the vihâra of the World-honoured one fell on the devâlaya of a contrary system; but when the sun was in the east, the shadow of that devâlaya was diverted to the north, and never fell on the vihâra of Buddha. The mal-believers regularly employed men to watch their devâlaya, to sweep and water (all about it), to burn incense, light the lamps, and present offerings; but in the morning the lamps were found to have been suddenly removed, and in the vihâra of Buddha. The Brahmans were indignant, and said, 'Those Śramaṇas take our lamps and use them for their own service of Buddha, but we will not stop our service for you[1]!' On that night the Brahmans themselves kept watch, when they saw the deva spirits which they served take the lamps and go three times round the vihâra of Buddha and present offerings. After this ministration to Buddha they suddenly disappeared. The Brahmans thereupon knowing how great was the spiritual power of Buddha, forthwith left their families, and became monks[2]. It has been handed down, that, near the time when these things occurred, around the Jetavana vihâra there were ninety-eight monasteries, in all

---

—a general name for all Brahmanical temples' (Eitel, p. 30). We read in the Khang-hsî dictionary under 寺, that when Kaśyapa Matanga came to the capital in the time of the emperor Ming of the second Han dynasty, from the Western Regions, with his Classics or Sûtras, he was lodged in the Court of State-Ceremonial, and that afterwards there was built for him 'The Court of the White-horse' (白 馬 寺), and in consequence the name of Sze (寺) came to be given to all Buddhistic temples. Fâ-hien, however, applies this term only to Brahmanical temples.

[1] Their speech was somewhat unconnected, but natural enough in the circumstances. Compare the whole account with the narrative in 1 Samuel v. about the Ark and Dagon, that 'twice-battered god of Palestine.'

[2] 'Entered the doctrine or path.' Three stages in the Buddhistic life are indicated by Fâ-hien:—'entering it,' as here, by becoming monks (入 道); 'getting it,' by becoming Arhats (得 道); and 'completing it,' by becoming Buddha (成 道).

of which there were monks residing, excepting only in one place which was vacant. In this Middle Kingdom [1] there are ninety-six [1] sorts of views, erroneous and different from our system, all of which recognise this world and the future world [2] (and the connexion between them). Each has its multitude of followers, and they all beg their food: only they do not carry the alms-bowl. They also, moreover, seek (to acquire) the blessing (of good deeds) on unfrequented ways, setting up on the road-side houses of charity, where rooms, couches, beds, and food and drink are supplied to travellers, and also to monks, coming and going as guests, the only difference being in the time (for which those parties remain).

There are also companies of the followers of Devadatta still existing. They regularly make offerings to the three previous Buddhas, but not to Śâkyamuni Buddha [3].

Four le south-east from the city of Śrâvastî, a tope has been

---

[1] It is not quite clear whether the author had in mind here Central India as a whole, which I think he had, or only Kośala, the part of it where he then was. In the older teaching, there were only thirty-two sects, but there may have been three subdivisions of each. See Rhys Davids' 'Buddhism,' pp. 98, 99.

[2] This mention of 'the future world' is an important difference between the Corean and Chinese texts. The want of it in the latter has been a stumbling-block in the way of all previous translators. Rémusat says in a note that 'the heretics limited themselves to speak of the duties of man in his actual life without connecting it by the notion of the metempsychosis with the anterior periods of existence through which he had passed.' But this is just the opposite of what Fâ-hien's meaning was, according to our Corean text. The notion of 'the metempsychosis' was just that in which all the ninety-six erroneous systems agreed among themselves and with Buddhism. If he had wished to say what the French sinologue thinks he does say, moreover, he would probably have written 皆知今世耳. Let me add, however, that the connexion which Buddhism holds between the past world (including the present) and the future is not that of a metempsychosis, or transmigration of souls, for it does not appear to admit any separate existence of the soul. Adhering to its own phraseology of 'the wheel,' I would call its doctrine that of 'The Transrotation of Births.' See Rhys Davids' third Hibbert Lecture.

[3] See p. 60, note 3; and p. 51, note 2.

erected at the place where the World-honoured one encountered king Virûdhaha[1], when he wished to attack the kingdom of Shay-e[1], and took his stand before him at the side of the road[2].

CHAPTER XXI.

THE THREE PREDECESSORS OF ŚÂKYAMUNI IN THE BUDDHASHIP.

FIFTY le to the west of the city bring (the traveller) to a town named Too-wei[3], the birthplace of Kâśyapa Buddha[3]. At the place where he and his father met[4], and at that where he attained to pari-nirvâṇa, topes were erected. Over the entire relic of the whole body of him, the Kâśyapa Tathâgata[5], a great tope was also erected.

---

[1] Or, more according to the phonetisation of the text, Vaidûrya. He was king of Kośala, the son and successor of Prasenajit, and the destroyer of Kapilavastu, the city of the Śâkya family. His hostility to the Śâkyas is sufficiently established, and it may be considered as certain that the name Shay-e, which, according to Julien's 'Méthode,' p. 89, may be read Chiâ-e, is the same as Kiâ-e (迦夷), one of the phonetisations of Kapilavastu, as given by Eitel.

[2] This would be the interview in the 'Life of the Buddha' in Trübner's Oriental Series, p. 116, when Virûdhaha on his march found Buddha under an old sakotato tree. It afforded him no shade; but he told the king that the thought of the danger of 'his relatives and kindred made it shady.' The king was moved to sympathy for the time, and went back to Śrâvastî; but the destruction of Kapilavastu was only postponed for a short space, and Buddha himself acknowledged it to be inevitable in the connexion of cause and effect.

[3] Identified, as Beal says, by Cunningham with Tadwa, a village nine miles to the west of Sâhara-mahat. The birthplace of Kâśyapa Buddha is generally thought to have been Benâres. According to a calculation of Rémusat, from his birth to A.D. 1832 there were 1,992,859 years!

[4] It seems to be necessary to have a meeting between every Buddha and his father. One at least is ascribed to Śâkyamuni and his father (real or supposed) Śuddhodana.

[5] This is the highest epithet given to every supreme Buddha; in Chinese 如來, meaning, as Eitel, p. 147, says, 'Sic profectus sum.' It is equivalent to 'Rightful Buddha, the true successor in the Supreme Buddha Line.' Hardy

Going on south-east from the city of Śrâvastî for twelve yojanas, (the travellers) came to a town named Na-pei-keâ[1], the birthplace of Krakuchanda Buddha[2]. At the place where he and his father met, and at that where he attained to pari-nirvâṇa, topes were erected. Going north from here less than a yojana, they came to a town which had been the birthplace of Kanakamuni Buddha[2]. At the place where he and his father met, and where he attained to pari-nirvâṇa, topes were erected.

CHAPTER XXII.

KAPILAVASTU. ITS DESOLATION. LEGENDS OF BUDDHA'S BIRTH, AND OTHER INCIDENTS IN CONNEXION WITH IT.

LESS than a yojana to the east from this brought them to the city of Kapilavastu[3]; but in it there was neither king nor people. All was mound and desolation. Of inhabitants there were only some monks and a score or two of families of the common people. At the spot where stood the old palace of king Śuddhodana[4] there have been made

---

concludes his account of the Kâśyapa Buddha (M. B., p. 97) with the following sentence:—'After his body was burnt, the bones still remained in their usual position, presenting the appearance of a perfect skeleton; and the whole of the inhabitants of Jambudvîpa, assembling together, erected a dagoba over his relics one yojana in height!'

[1] Na-pei-keâ or Nabhiga is not mentioned elsewhere. Eitel says this Buddha was born at the city of Gân-ho (安 和 城), and Hardy gives his birthplace as Mekhala. It may be possible, by means of Sanskrit, to reconcile these statements.

[2] See note 2, p. 51.

[3] Kapilavastu, 'the city of beautiful virtue,' was the birthplace of Śâkyamuni, but was destroyed, as intimated in the notes on last chapter, during his lifetime. It was situated a short distance north-west of the present Goruckpoor, lat. 26° 46′ N., lon. 83° 19′ E. Davids says (Manual, p. 25), 'It was on the banks of the river Rohini, the modern Kohana, about 100 miles north-west of the city of Benâres.'

[4] The father, or supposed father, of Śâkyamuni. He is here called 'the king white and pure' (白 淨 王). A more common appellation is 'the king of pure

I. DREAM OF BUDDHA'S MOTHER OF HIS INCARNATION. Ch. 22.

images of the prince (his eldest son) and his mother[1]; and at the places where that son appeared mounted on a white elephant when he entered his mother's womb[2], and where he turned his carriage round on seeing the sick man after he had gone out of the city by the eastern gate[3], topes have been erected. The places (were also pointed out)[4] where (the ṛishi) Â-e[5] inspected the marks[6] (of Buddhaship on the body) of the heir-apparent (when an infant); where, when he was in company with Nanda and others, on the elephant being struck down and drawn on one side, he tossed it away[7]; where he shot an arrow to the south-east, and it

---

rice (淨飯王);' but the character 飯, or 'rice,' must be a mistake for 梵, 'Brahman,' and the appellation='Pure Brahman king.'

[1] The 'eldest son' or 'prince' was Śâkyamuni, and his mother had no other son. For 'his mother,' see note 2, page 48. She was a daughter of Añjana or Anuśâkya, king of the neighbouring country of Koli, and Yaśodharâ, an aunt of Śuddhodana. There appear to have been various intermarriages between the royal houses of Kapila and Koli.

[2] In 'The Life of the Buddha,' p. 15, we read that 'Buddha was now in the Tushita heaven, and knowing that his time was come (the time for his last rebirth in the course of which he would become Buddha), he made the necessary examinations; and having decided that Mahâ-mâyâ was the right mother, in the midnight watch he entered her womb under the appearance of an elephant.' See M. B., pp. 140–143, and, still better, Rhys Davids' 'Birth Stories,' pp. 58–63.

[3] In Hardy's M. B., pp. 154, 155, we read, 'As the prince (Siddhârtha, the first name given to Śâkyamuni; see Eitel, under Sarvârthasiddha) was one day passing along, he saw a deva under the appearance of a leper, full of sores, with a body like a water-vessel, and legs like the pestle for pounding rice; and when he learned from his charioteer what it was that he saw, he became agitated, and returned at once to the palace.' See also Rhys Davids' 'Buddhism,' p. 29.

[4] This is an addition of my own, instead of 'There are also topes erected at the following spots' of former translators. Fâ-hien does not say there were memorial topes at all these places.

[5] Asita; see Eitel, p. 15. He is called in Pâli Kalâ Devala, and had been a minister of Śuddhodana's father.

[6] See note 2, page 39.

[7] In 'The Life of the Buddha' we read that the Lichchhavis of Vaiśâlî had sent to the young prince a very fine elephant; but when it was near Kapilavastu, Devadatta,

went a distance of thirty le, then entering the ground and making a spring to come forth, which men subsequently fashioned into a well from which travellers might drink[1]; where, after he had attained to Wisdom[2], Buddha returned and saw the king, his father[3]; where five hundred Śâkyas quitted their families and did reverence to Upâli[4] while the earth shook and moved in six different ways; where Buddha preached his Law to the devas, and the four deva kings and others kept the four doors (of the hall), so that (even) the king, his father, could not enter[5]; where Buddha sat under a nyagrodha tree, which is still standing[6], with his face to the east, and (his aunt) Mahâ-prajâpatî presented him with a

---

out of envy, killed it with a blow of his fist. Nanda (not Ânanda, but a half-brother of Siddhârtha), coming that way, saw the carcase lying on the road, and pulled it on one side; but the Bodhisattva, seeing it there, took it by the tail, and tossed it over seven fences and ditches, when the force of its fall made a great ditch. I suspect that the characters in the column have been disarranged, and that we should read 樸 捅 象 處, 射 箭, 云 云. Buddha, that is Siddhârtha, was at this time only ten years old.

[1] The young Śâkyas were shooting when the prince thus surpassed them all. He was then seventeen.

[2] See note 2, page 61.

[3] This was not the night when he finally fled from Kapilavastu, and as he was leaving the palace, perceived his sleeping father, and said, 'Father, though I love thee, yet a fear possesses me, and I may not stay;'—The Life of the Buddha, p. 25. Most probably it was that related in M. B., pp. 199–204. See 'Buddhist Birth Stories,' pp. 120–127.

[4] They did this, I suppose, to show their humility, for Upâli was only a Śûdra by birth, and had been a barber; so from the first did Buddhism assert its superiority to the conditions of rank and caste. Upâli was distinguished by his knowledge of the rules of discipline, and praised on that account by Buddha. He was one of the three leaders of the first synod, and the principal compiler of the original Vinaya books.

[5] I have not met with the particulars of this preaching.

[6] Meaning, as explained in Chinese, 'a tree without knots;' the ficus Indica. See Rhys Davids' note, Manual, p. 39, where he says that a branch of one of these trees was taken from Buddha Gayâ to Anurâdhapura in Ceylon in the middle of the third century B. C., and is still growing there, the oldest historical tree in the world.

III. BUDDHA TOSSING THE ELEPHANT OVER THE WALL. Ch. 22.

II. BUDDHA JUST BORN, WITH THE NAGAS SUPPLYING WATER TO WASH HIM. Ch. 22.

Saṅghâli[1]; and (where) king Vaidûrya slew the seed of Śâkya, and they all in dying became Śrotâpannas[2]. A tope was erected at this last place, which is still existing.

Several le north-east from the city was the king's field, where the heir-apparent sat under a tree, and looked at the ploughers[3].

Fifty le east from the city was a garden, named Lumbinî[4], where the queen entered the pond and bathed. Having come forth from the pond on the northern bank, after (walking) twenty paces, she lifted up her hand, laid hold of a branch of a tree, and, with her face to the east, gave birth to the heir-apparent[5]. When he fell to the ground, he (immediately) walked seven paces. Two dragon-kings (appeared) and washed his body. At the place where they did so, there was immediately formed a well, and from it, as well as from the above pond, where (the queen) bathed[6], the monks (even) now constantly take the water, and drink it.

---

[1] See note 1, page 39. I have not met with the account of this presentation. See the long account of Prajâpatî in M. B., pp. 306–315.

[2] See note 2, page 57. The Śrotâpannas are the first class of saints, who are not to be reborn in a lower sphere, but attain to nirvâṇa after having been reborn seven times consecutively as men or devas. The Chinese editions state there were '1000' of the Śâkya seed. The general account is that they were 500, all maidens, who refused to take their place in king Vaidûrya's harem, and were in consequence taken to a pond, and had their hands and feet cut off. There Buddha came to them, had their wounds dressed, and preached to them the Law. They died in the faith, and were reborn in the region of the four Great Kings. Thence they came back and visited Buddha at Jetavana in the night, and there they obtained the reward of Śrotâpanna. 'The Life of the Buddha,' p. 121.

[3] See the account of this in M. B., p. 150. The account of it reminds me of the ploughing by the sovereign, which has been an institution in China from the earliest times. But there we have no magic and no extravagance.

[4] 'The place of Liberation;' see note 2, page 38.

[5] See the accounts of this event in M. B., pp. 145, 146; 'The Life of the Buddha,' pp. 15, 16; and 'Buddhist Birth Stories,' p. 66.

[6] There is difficulty in construing the text of this last statement. Mr. Beal had, no doubt inadvertently, omitted it in his first translation. In his revised version he gives for it, I cannot say happily, 'As well as at the pool, the water of which came down from above for washing (the child).'

There are four places of regular and fixed occurrence (in the history of) all Buddhas:—first, the place where they attained to perfect Wisdom (and became Buddha); second, the place where they turned the wheel of the Law[1]; third, the place where they preached the Law, discoursed of righteousness, and discomfited (the advocates of) erroneous doctrines; and fourth, the place where they came down, after going up to the Trayastriṃśas heaven to preach the Law for the benefit of their mothers. Other places in connexion with them became remarkable, according to the manifestations which were made at them at particular times.

The country of Kapilavastu is a great scene of empty desolation. The inhabitants are few and far between. On the roads people have to be on their guard against white elephants[2] and lions, and should not travel incautiously.

CHAPTER XXIII.

RÂMA, AND ITS TOPE.

EAST from Buddha's birthplace, and at a distance of five yojanas, there is a kingdom called Râma[3]. The king of this country, having obtained one portion of the relics of Buddha's body[4], returned with it and built over it a tope, named the Râma tope. By the side of it there was a pool, and in the pool a dragon, which constantly kept watch over (the tope), and presented offerings at it day and night. When king Aśoka

[1] See note 3, page 49. See also Davids' Manual, p. 45. The latter says, that 'to turn the wheel of the Law' means 'to set rolling the royal chariot wheel of a universal empire of truth and righteousness;' but he admits that this is more grandiloquent than the phraseology was in the ears of Buddhists. I prefer the words quoted from Eitel in the note referred to. 'They turned' is probably equivalent to 'They began to turn.'

[2] Fâ-hien does not say that he himself saw any of these white elephants, nor does he speak of the lions as of any particular colour. We shall find by-and-by, in a note further on, that, to make them appear more terrible, they are spoken of as 'black.'

[3] Râma or Râmagrâma, between Kapilavastu and Kuśanagara.

[4] See the account of the eightfold division of the relics of Buddha's body in the Sacred Books of the East, vol. xi, Buddhist Suttas, pp. 133–136.

came forth into the world, he wished to destroy the eight topes (over the relics), and to build (instead of them) 84,000 topes[1]. After he had thrown down the seven (others), he wished next to destroy this tope. But then the dragon showed itself, took the king into its palace[2]; and when he had seen all the things provided for offerings, it said to him, 'If you are able with your offerings to exceed these, you can destroy the tope, and take it all away. I will not contend with you.' The king, however, knew that such appliances for offerings were not to be had anywhere in the world, and thereupon returned (without carrying out his purpose).

(Afterwards), the ground all about became overgrown with vegetation, and there was nobody to sprinkle and sweep (about the tope); but a herd of elephants came regularly, which brought water with their trunks to water the ground, and various kinds of flowers and incense, which they presented at the tope. (Once) there came from one of the kingdoms a devotee[3] to worship at the tope. When he encountered the elephants he was greatly alarmed, and screened himself among the trees; but when he saw them go through with the offerings in the most proper manner, the thought filled him with great sadness—that there should be no monastery here, (the inmates of which) might serve the tope, but the elephants have to do the watering and sweeping. Forthwith he gave up the great prohibitions (by which he was bound)[4], and resumed the status of a Śrâmaṇera[5]. With his own hands he cleared away the grass and trees, put the place in good order, and made it pure and clean. By the power of his exhortations, he prevailed on the king of the country to

---

[1] The bones of the human body are supposed to consist of 84,000 atoms, and hence the legend of Aśoka's wish to build 84,000 topes, one over each atom of Śâkyamuni's skeleton.

[2] Fâ-hien, it appears to me, intended his readers to understand that the nâga-guardian had a palace of his own, inside or underneath the pool or tank.

[3] It stands out on the narrative as a whole that we have not here 'some pilgrims,' but one devotee.

[4] What the 'great prohibitions' which the devotee now gave up were we cannot tell. Being what he was, a monk of more than ordinary ascetical habits, he may have undertaken peculiar and difficult vows.

[5] The Śrâmaṇera, or in Chinese Shâmei. See note 7, page 45.

form a residence for monks; and when that was done, he became head of the monastery. At the present day there are monks residing in it. This event is of recent occurrence; but in all the succession from that time till now, there has always been a Śrâmaṇera head of the establishment.

CHAPTER XXIV.

WHERE BUDDHA FINALLY RENOUNCED THE WORLD, AND WHERE HE DIED.

EAST from here four yojanas, there is the place where the heir-apparent sent back Chaṇḍaka, with his white horse[1]; and there also a tope was erected.

Four yojanas to the east from this, (the travellers) came to the Charcoal tope[2], where there is also a monastery.

Going on twelve yojanas, still to the east, they came to the city of Kuśanagara[3], on the north of which, between two trees[4], on the bank of the Nairañjanâ[5] river, is the place where the World-honoured one, with his head to the north, attained to pari-nirvâṇa (and died). There

---

[1] This was on the night when Śâkyamuni finally left his palace and family to fulfil the course to which he felt that he was called. Chaṇḍaka, in Pâli Channa, was the prince's charioteer, and in sympathy with him. So also was the white horse Kanthaka (Kanthakanam Aśvarâja), which neighed his delight till the devas heard him. See M. B., pp. 158–161, and Davids' Manual, pp. 32, 33. According to 'Buddhist Birth Stories,' p. 87, the noble horse never returned to the city, but died of grief at being left by his master, to be reborn immediately in the Trayastriṃśas heaven as the deva Kanthaka!

[2] Beal and Giles call this the 'Ashes' tope. I also would have preferred to call it so; but the Chinese character is 炭, not 灰. Rémusat has 'la tour des charbons.' It was over the place of Buddha's cremation.

[3] In Pâli Kusinârâ. It got its name from the Kuśa grass (the poa cynosuroides); and its ruins are still extant, near Kusiah, 180 N.W. from Patna; 'about,' says Davids, '120 miles N. N. E. of Benâres, and 80 miles due east of Kapilavastu.'

[4] The Śâla tree, the Shorea robusta, which yields the famous teak wood.

[5] Confounded, according to Eitel, even by Hsüan-chwang, with the Hiraṇyavatî, which flows past the city on the south.

VII. BUDDHA'S DYING INSTRUCTIONS. Ch. 24.

VIII. BUDDHA'S DEATH. Ch. 24.

IX. DIVISION OF BUDDHA'S RELICS. Ch. 24.

also are the places where Subhadra[1], the last (of his converts), attained to Wisdom (and became an Arhat); where in his coffin of gold they made offerings to the World-honoured one for seven days[2], where the Vajrapâṇi laid aside his golden club[3], and where the eight kings divided the relics (of the burnt body)[4]:—at all these places were built topes and monasteries, all of which are now existing.

In the city the inhabitants are few and far between, comprising only the families belonging to the (different) societies of monks.

Going from this to the south-east for twelve yojanas, they came to the place where the Lichchhavis[5] wished to follow Buddha to (the

---

[1] A Brahman of Benâres, said to have been 120 years old, who came to learn from Buddha the very night he died. Ânanda would have repulsed him; but Buddha ordered him to be introduced; and then putting aside the ingenious but unimportant question which he propounded, preached to him the Law. The Brahman was converted and attained at once to Arhatship. Eitel says that he attained to nirvâṇa a few moments before Śâkyamuni; but see the full account of him and his conversion in 'Buddhist Suttas,' pp. 103–110.

[2] Thus treating the dead Buddha as if he had been a Chakravartti king. Hardy's M. B., p. 347, says:—'For the place of cremation, the princes (of Kuśinâra) offered their own coronation-hall, which was decorated with the utmost magnificence, and the body was deposited in a golden sarcophagus.' See the account of a cremation which Fâ-hien witnessed in Ceylon, chap. xxxix.

[3] The name Vajrapâṇi is explained as 'he who holds in his hand the diamond club (or pestle=sceptre),' which is one of the many names of Indra or Śakra. He therefore, that great protector of Buddhism, would seem to be intended here; but the difficulty with me is that neither in Hardy nor Rockhill, nor any other writer, have I met with any manifestation of himself made by Indra on this occasion. The princes of Kuśanagara were called mallas, 'strong or mighty heroes;' so also were those of Pâvâ and Vaiśâlî; and a question arises whether the language may not refer to some story which Fâ-hien had heard,—something which they did on this great occasion. Vajrapâṇi is also explained as meaning 'the diamond mighty hero;' but the epithet of 'diamond' is not so applicable to them as to Indra. The clause may hereafter obtain more elucidation.

[4] Of Kuśanagara, Pâvâ, Vaiśâlî, and other kingdoms. Kings, princes, brahmans,—each wanted the whole relic; but they agreed to an eightfold division at the suggestion of the brahman Droṇa.

[5] These 'strong heroes' were the chiefs of Vaiśâlî, a kingdom and city, with

place of) his pari-nirvâṇa, and where, when he would not listen to them and they kept cleaving to him, unwilling to go away, he made to appear a large and deep ditch which they could not cross over, and gave them his alms-bowl, as a pledge of his regard, (thus) sending them back to their families. There a stone pillar was erected with an account of this event engraved upon it.

CHAPTER XXV.

VAIŚÂLÎ. THE TOPE CALLED 'WEAPONS LAID DOWN.' THE COUNCIL OF VAIŚÂLÎ.

EAST from this city ten yojanas, (the travellers) came to the kingdom of Vaiśâlî. North of the city so named is a large forest, having in it the double-galleried vihâra [1] where Buddha dwelt, and the tope over half the body of Ânanda [2]. Inside the city the woman Âmbapâlî [3] built a vihâra in honour of Buddha, which is now standing as it was at first. Three le south of the city, on the west of the road, (is the) garden (which) the same Âmbapâlî presented to Buddha, in which he might

---

an oligarchical constitution. They embraced Buddhism early, and were noted for their peculiar attachment to Buddha. The second synod was held at Vaiśâlî, as related in the next chapter. The ruins of the city still exist at Bassahar, north of Patna, the same, I suppose, as Besarh, twenty miles north of Hajipûr. See Beal's Revised Version, p. lii.

[1] It is difficult to tell what was the peculiar form of this vihâra from which it got its name; something about the construction of its door, or cupboards, or galleries.

[2] See the explanation of this in the next chapter.

[3] Âmbapâlî, Âmrapâlî, or Âmradarikâ, 'the guardian of the Âmra (probably the mango) tree,' is famous in Buddhist annals. See the account of her in M. B., pp. 456–8. She was a courtesan. She had been in many nârakas or hells, was 100,000 times a female beggar, and 10,000 times a prostitute; but maintaining perfect continence during the period of Kâśyapa Buddha, Śâkyamuni's predecessor, she had been born a devî, and finally appeared in earth under an Âmra tree in Vaiśâlî. There again she fell into her old ways, and had a son by king Bimbisâra; but she was won over by Buddha to virtue and chastity, renounced the world, and attained to the state of an Ârhat. See the earliest account of Âmbapâlî's presentation of the garden in 'Buddhist Suttas,' pp. 30–33, and the note there from Bishop Bigandet on pp. 33, 34.

reside. When Buddha was about to attain to his pari-nirvâṇa, as he was quitting the city by the west gate, he turned round, and, beholding the city on his right, said to them, 'Here I have taken my last walk[1].' Men subsequently built a tope at this spot.

Three le north-west of the city there is a tope called, 'Bows and weapons laid down.' The reason why it got that name was this:—The inferior wife of a king, whose country lay along the river Ganges, brought forth from her womb a ball of flesh. The superior wife, jealous of the other, said, 'You have brought forth a thing of evil omen,' and immediately it was put into a box of wood and thrown into the river. Farther down the stream another king was walking and looking about, when he saw the wooden box (floating) in the water. (He had it brought to him), opened it, and found a thousand little boys, upright and complete, and each one different from the others. He took them and had them brought up. They grew tall and large, and very daring and strong, crushing all opposition in every expedition which they undertook. By and by they attacked the kingdom of their real father, who became in consequence greatly distressed and sad. His inferior wife asked what it was that made him so, and he replied, 'That king has a thousand sons, daring and strong beyond compare, and he wishes with them to attack my kingdom; this is what makes me sad.' The wife said, 'You need not be sad and sorrowful. Only make a high gallery on the wall of the city on the east; and when the thieves come, I shall be able to make them retire.' The king did as she said; and when the enemies came, she said to them from the tower, 'You are my sons; why are you acting so unnaturally and rebelliously?' They replied, 'Who are you that say you are our mother?' 'If you do not believe me,' she said, 'look, all of you, towards me, and open your mouths.' She then pressed her breasts with her two hands, and each sent forth 500 jets of milk, which fell into the mouths of the thousand sons. The thieves (thus) knew that she was their mother, and laid down their bows and weapons[2]. The two kings, the fathers,

---

[1] Beal gives, 'In this place I have performed the last religious act of my earthly career;' Giles, 'This is the last place I shall visit;' Rémusat, 'C'est un lieu où je reviendrai bien longtemps après ceci.' Perhaps the 'walk' to which Buddha referred had been for meditation.

[2] See the account of this legend in the note in M. B., pp. 235, 236, different, but

hereupon fell into reflection, and both got to be Pratyeka Buddhas[1]. The tope of the two Pratyeka Buddhas is still existing.

In a subsequent age, when the World-honoured one had attained to perfect Wisdom (and become Buddha), he said to his disciples, 'This is the place where I in a former age laid down my bow and weapons[2].' It was thus that subsequently men got to know (the fact), and raised the tope on this spot, which in this way received its name. The thousand little boys were the thousand Buddhas of this Bhadra-kalpa[3].

It was by the side of the 'Weapons-laid-down' tope that Buddha, having given up the idea of living longer, said to Ânanda, 'In three months from this I will attain to pari-nirvâṇa;' and king Mâra[4] had so fascinated and stupefied Ânanda, that he was not able to ask Buddha to remain longer in this world.

Three or four le east from this place there is a tope (commemorating

---

not less absurd. The first part of Fâ-hien's narrative will have sent the thoughts of some of my readers to the exposure of the infant Moses, as related in Exodus.

[1] See note 3, page 40.

[2] Thus Śâkyamuni had been one of the thousand little boys who floated in the box in the Ganges. How long back the former age was we cannot tell. I suppose the tope of the two fathers who became Pratyeka Buddhas had been built like the one commemorating the laying down of weapons after Buddha had told his disciples of the strange events in the past.

[3] Bhadra-kalpa, 'the Kalpa of worthies or sages.' 'This,' says Eitel, p. 22, 'is a designation for a Kalpa of stability, so called because 1000 Buddhas appear in the course of it. Our present period is a Bhadra-kalpa, and four Buddhas have already appeared. It is to last 236 millions of years, but over 151 millions have already elapsed.'

[4] 'The king of demons.' The name Mâra is explained by 'the murderer,' 'the destroyer of virtue,' and similar appellations. 'He is,' says Eitel, 'the personification of lust, the god of love, sin, and death, the arch-enemy of goodness, residing in the heaven Paranirmita Vaśavartin on the top of the Kâmadhâtu. He assumes different forms, especially monstrous ones, to tempt or frighten the saints, or sends his daughters, or inspires wicked men like Devadatta or the Nirgranthas to do his work. He is often represented with 100 arms, and riding on an elephant.' The oldest form of the legend in this paragraph is in 'Buddhist Suttas,' Sacred Books of the East, vol. xi, pp. 41–55, where Buddha says that, if Ânanda had asked him thrice, he would have postponed his death.

the following occurrence):—A hundred years after the pari-nirvâṇa of Buddha, some Bhikshus of Vaiśâlî went wrong in the matter of the disciplinary rules in ten particulars, and appealed for their justification to what they said were the words of Buddha. Hereupon the Arhats and Bhikshus observant of the rules, to the number in all of 700 monks, examined afresh and collated the collection of disciplinary books[1]. Subsequently men built at this place the tope (in question), which is still existing.

CHAPTER XXVI.

REMARKABLE DEATH OF ÂNANDA.

FOUR yojanas on from this place to the east brought the travellers to the confluence of the five rivers[2]. When Ânanda was going from Magadha[3] to Vaiśâlî, wishing his pari-nirvâṇa to take place (there), the

---

[1] Or the Vinaya-piṭaka. The meeting referred to was an important one, and is generally spoken of as the second Great Council of the Buddhist Church. See, on the formation of the Buddhist Canon, Hardy's E. M., chap. xviii, and the last chapter of Davids' Manual, on the History of the Order. The first Council was that held at Râjagṛiha, shortly after Buddha's death, under the presidency of Kâśyapa;—say about B.C. 410. The second was that spoken of here;—say about B.C. 300. In Davids' Manual (p. 216) we find the ten points of discipline, in which the heretics (I can use that term here) claimed at least indulgence. Two meetings were held to consider and discuss them. At the former the orthodox party barely succeeded in carrying their condemnation of the laxer monks; and a second and larger meeting, of which Fâ-hien speaks, was held in consequence, and a more emphatic condemnation passed. At the same time all the books and subjects of discipline seem to have undergone a careful revision.

The Corean text is clearer than the Chinese as to those who composed the Council,—the Arhats and orthodox monks. The leader among them was a Yaśas, or Yaśada, or Yedśaputtra, who had been a disciple of Ânanda, and must therefore have been a very old man.

[2] This spot does not appear to have been identified. It could not be far from Patna.

[3] Magadha was for some time the headquarters of Buddhism; the holy land, covered with vihâras; a fact perpetuated, as has been observed in a previous

devas informed king Ajâtaśatru[1] of it, and the king immediately pursued him, in his own grand carriage, with a body of soldiers, and had reached the river. (On the other hand), the Lichchhavis of Vaiśâlî had heard that Ânanda was coming (to their city), and they on their part came to meet him. (In this way), they all arrived together at the river, and Ânanda considered that, if he went forward, king Ajâtaśatru would be very angry, while, if he went back, the Lichchhavis would resent his conduct. He thereupon in the very middle of the river burnt his body in a fiery ecstasy of Samâdhi[2], and his pari-nirvâṇa was attained. He divided

---

note, in the name of the present Behâr, the southern portion of which corresponds to the ancient kingdom of Magadha.

[1] In Singhalese, Ajasat. See the account of his conversion in M. B., pp. 321–326. He was the son of king Bimbisâra, who was one of the first royal converts to Buddhism. Ajasat murdered his father, or at least wrought his death; and was at first opposed to Śâkyamuni, and a favourer of Devadatta. When converted, he became famous for his liberality in almsgiving.

[2] Eitel has a long article (pp. 114, 115) on the meaning of Samâdhi, which is one of the seven sections of wisdom (bodhyanga). Hardy defines it as meaning 'perfect tranquillity;' Turnour, as 'meditative abstraction;' Burnouf, as 'self-control;' and Edkins, as 'ecstatic reverie.' 'Samâdhi,' says Eitel, 'signifies the highest pitch of abstract, ecstatic meditation; a state of absolute indifference to all influences from within or without; a state of torpor of both the material and spiritual forces of vitality; a sort of terrestrial nirvâṇa, consistently culminating in total destruction of life.' He then quotes apparently the language of the text, 'He consumed his body by Agni (the fire of) Samâdhi,' and says it is 'a common expression for the effects of such ecstatic, ultra-mystic self-annihilation.' All this is simply 'a darkening of counsel by words without knowledge.' Some facts concerning the death of Ânanda are hidden beneath the darkness of the phraseology, which it is impossible for us to ascertain. By or in Samâdhi he burns his body in the very middle of the river, and then he divides the relic of the burnt body into two parts (for so evidently Fâ-hien intended his narration to be taken), and leaves one half on each bank. The account of Ânanda's death in Nien-ch'ang's 'History of Buddha and the Patriarchs' is much more extravagant. Crowds of men and devas are brought together to witness it. The body is divided into four parts. One is conveyed to the Tushita heaven; a second, to the palace of a certain Nâga king; a third is given to Ajâtaśatru; and the fourth to the Lichchhavis. What it all really means I cannot tell.

his body (also) into two, (leaving) the half of it on each bank; so that each of the two kings got one half as a (sacred) relic, and took it back (to his own capital), and there raised a tope over it.

CHAPTER XXVII.

PÂṬALIPUTTRA OR PATNA, IN MAGADHA. KING AŚOKA'S SPIRIT-BUILT PALACE AND HALLS. THE BUDDHIST BRAHMAN, RÂDHA-SÂMI. DISPENSARIES AND HOSPITALS.

HAVING crossed the river, and descended south for a yojana, (the travellers) came to the town of Pâṭaliputtra[1], in the kingdom of Magadha, the city where king Aśoka[2] ruled. The royal palace and halls in the midst of the city, which exist now as of old, were all made by spirits which he employed, and which piled up the stones, reared the walls and gates, and executed the elegant carving and inlaid sculpture-work,—in a way which no human hands of this world could accomplish.

King Aśoka had a younger brother who had attained to be an Arhat, and resided on Gṛidhra-kûṭa[3] hill, finding his delight in solitude and quiet. The king, who sincerely reverenced him, wished and begged him (to come and live) in his family, where he could supply all his wants. The other, however, through his delight in the stillness of the mountain, was unwilling to accept the invitation, on which the king said to him, 'Only accept my invitation, and I will make a hill for you inside the city.' Accordingly, he provided the materials of a feast,

---

[1] The modern Patna, lat. 25° 28′ N., lon. 85° 15′ E. The Sanskrit name means 'The city of flowers.' It is the Indian Florence.

[2] See note 5, page 31. Aśoka transferred his court from Râjagṛiha to Pâṭaliputtra, and there, in the eighteenth year of his reign, he convoked the third Great Synod,—according, at least, to southern Buddhism. It must have been held a few years before B.C. 250; Eitel says in 246.

[3] 'The Vulture-hill;' so called because Mâra, according to Buddhist tradition, once assumed the form of a vulture on it to interrupt the meditation of Ânanda; or, more probably, because it was a resort of vultures. It was near Râjagṛiha, the earlier capital of Aśoka, so that Fâ-hien connects a legend of it with his account of Patna. It abounded in caverns, and was famous as a resort of ascetics.

called to him the spirits, and announced to them, 'To-morrow you will all receive my invitation; but as there are no mats for you to sit on, let each one bring (his own seat).' Next day the spirits came, each one bringing with him a great rock, (like) a wall, four or five paces square, (for a seat). When their sitting was over, the king made them form a hill with the large stones piled on one another, and also at the foot of the hill, with five large square stones, to make an apartment, which might be more than thirty cubits long, twenty cubits wide, and more than ten cubits high.

In this city there had resided a great Brahman[1], named Râdha-sâmi[2], a professor of the mahâyâna, of clear discernment and much wisdom, who understood everything, living by himself in spotless purity. The king of the country honoured and reverenced him, and served him as his teacher. If he went to inquire for and greet him, the king did not presume to sit down alongside of him; and if, in his love and reverence, he took hold of his hand, as soon as he let it go, the Brahman made haste to pour water on it and wash it. He might be more than fifty years old, and all the kingdom looked up to him. By means of this one man, the Law of Buddha was widely made known, and the followers of other doctrines did not find it in their power to persecute the body of monks in any way.

By the side of the tope of Aśoka, there has been made a mahâyâna monastery, very grand and beautiful; there is also a hînayâna one; the two together containing six hundred or seven hundred monks. The rules of demeanour and the scholastic arrangements[3] in them are worthy of observation.

Shamans of the highest virtue from all quarters, and students, inquirers

---

[1] A Brahman by caste, but a Buddhist in faith.

[2] So, by the help of Julien's 'Méthode,' I transliterate the Chinese characters 羅太私迷. Beal gives Râdhasvâmi, his Chinese text having a 婆 between 私 and 迷. I suppose the name was Râdhasvâmi or Râdhasâmi.

[3] 庠序, the names of two kinds of schools, often occurring in the Lî Kî and Mencius. Why should there not have been schools in those monasteries in India as there were in China? Fâ-hien himself grew up with other boys in a monastery, and no doubt had to 'go to school.' And the next sentence shows us there might be schools for more advanced students as well as for the Śrâmaṇeras.

wishing to find out truth and the grounds of it, all resort to these monasteries. There also resides in this monastery a Brahman teacher, whose name also is Mañjuśrî[1], whom the Shamans of greatest virtue in the kingdom, and the mahâyâna Bhikshus honour and look up to.

The cities and towns of this country are the greatest of all in the Middle Kingdom. The inhabitants are rich and prosperous, and vie with one another in the practice of benevolence and righteousness. Every year on the eighth day of the second month they celebrate a procession of images. They make a four-wheeled car, and on it erect a structure of five storeys by means of bamboos tied together. This is supported by a king-post, with poles and lances slanting from it, and is rather more than twenty cubits high, having the shape of a tope. White and silk-like cloth of hair[2] is wrapped all round it, which is then painted in various colours. They make figures of devas, with gold, silver, and lapis lazuli grandly blended and having silken streamers and canopies hung out over them. On the four sides are niches, with a Buddha seated in each, and a Bodhisattva standing in attendance on him. There may be twenty cars, all grand and imposing, but each one different from the others. On the day mentioned, the monks and laity within the borders all come together; they have singers and skilful musicians; they pay their devotions with flowers and incense. The Brahmans come and invite the Buddhas to enter the city. These do so in order, and remain two nights in it. All through the night they keep lamps burning, have skilful music, and present offerings. This is the practice in all the other kingdoms as well. The Heads of the Vaiśya families in them establish in the cities houses for dispensing charity and medicines. All the poor and destitute in the country, orphans, widowers, and childless men, maimed people and cripples, and all who are diseased, go to those houses, and are provided with every kind of help, and doctors examine their diseases. They get the food and medicines which their cases require, and are made to feel at ease; and when they are better, they go away of themselves.

When king Aśoka destroyed the seven topes, (intending) to make

---

[1] See note 1, page 4. It is perhaps with reference to the famous Bodhisattva that the Brahman here is said to be 'also' named Mañjuśrî.

[2] ? Cashmere cloth.

eighty-four thousand[1], the first which he made was the great tope, more than three le to the south of this city. In front of this there is a footprint of Buddha, where a vihâra has been built. The door of it faces the north, and on the south of it there is a stone pillar, fourteen or fifteen cubits in circumference, and more than thirty cubits high, on which there is an inscription, saying, 'Aśoka gave the jambudvîpa to the general body of all the monks, and then redeemed it from them with money. This he did three times[2].' North from the tope 300 or 400 paces, king Aśoka built the city of Ne-le[3]. In it there is a stone pillar, which also is more than thirty feet high, with a lion on the top of it. On the pillar there is an inscription recording the things which led to the building of Ne-le, with the number of the year, the day, and the month.

CHAPTER XXVIII.

RÂJAGṚIHA, NEW AND OLD. LEGENDS AND INCIDENTS CONNECTED WITH IT.

(THE travellers) went on from this to the south-east for nine yojanas, and came to a small solitary rocky hill[4], at the head or end of which[5] was an apartment of stone, facing the south,—the place where Buddha sat, when Śakra, Ruler of Devas, brought the deva-musician, Pañcha-

---

[1] See note 1, page 69.

[2] We wish that we had more particulars of this great transaction, and that we knew what value in money Aśoka set on the whole world. It is to be observed that he gave it to the monks, and did not receive it from them. Their right was from him, and he bought it back. He was the only 'Power' that was.

[3] We know nothing more of Ne-le. It could only have been a small place; an outpost for the defence of Pâṭaliputtra.

[4] Called by Hsüan-chwang Indra-śila-guhâ, or 'The cavern of Indra.' It has been identified with a hill near the village of Giryek, on the bank of the Pañchâna river, about thirty-six miles from Gayâ. The hill terminates in two peaks overhanging the river, and it is the more northern and higher of these which Fâ-hien had in mind. It bears an oblong terrace covered with the ruins of several buildings, especially of a vihâra.

[5] This does not mean the top or summit of the hill, but its 'headland,' where it ended at the river.

(śikha)[1], to give pleasure to him by playing on his lute. Śakra then asked Buddha about forty-two subjects, tracing (the questions) out with his finger one by one on the rock[2]. The prints of his tracing are still there; and here also there is a monastery.

A yojana south-west from this place brought them to the village of Nâla[3], where Śâriputtra[4] was born, and to which also he returned, and attained here his pari-nirvâṇa. Over the spot (where his body was burned) there was built a tope, which is still in existence.

Another yojana to the west brought them to New Râjagṛiha[5],—the new city which was built by king Ajâtaśatru. There were two monasteries in it. Three hundred paces outside the west gate, king Ajâtaśatru, having obtained one portion of the relics of Buddha, built (over them) a tope, high, large, grand, and beautiful. Leaving the city by the south gate, and proceeding south four le, one enters a valley, and comes to a circular space formed by five hills, which stand all round

---

[1] See the account of this visit of Śakra in M. B., pp. 288–290. It is from Hardy that we are able to complete here the name of the musician, which appears in Fâ-hien as only Pañcha, or 'Five.' His harp or lute, we are told, was 'twelve miles long.'

[2] Hardy (M. B., pp. 288, 289) makes the subjects only thirteen, which are still to be found in one of the Sûtras ('the Dik-Saṅga, in the Śakra-praśna Sûtra'). Whether it was Śakra who wrote his questions, or Buddha who wrote the answers, depends on the punctuation. It seems better to make Śakra the writer.

[3] Or Nâlanda; identified with the present Baragong. A grand monastery was subsequently built at it, famous by the residence for five years of Hsüan-chwang.

[4] See note 3, page 44. There is some doubt as to the statement that Nâla was his birthplace.

[5] The city of 'Royal Palaces;' 'the residence of the Magadha kings from Bimbisâra to Aśoka, the first metropolis of Buddhism, at the foot of the Gṛidhrakûṭa mountains. Here the first synod assembled within a year after Śâkyamuni's death. Its ruins are still extant at the village of Rajghir, sixteen miles S.W. of Behâr, and form an object of pilgrimage to the Jains (E. H., p. 100).' It is called New Râjagṛiha to distinguish it from Kuśâgârapura, a few miles from it, the old residence of the kings. Eitel says it was built by Bimbisâra, while Fâ-hien ascribes it to Ajâtaśatru. I suppose the son finished what the father had begun.

it, and have the appearance of the suburban wall of a city. Here was the old city of king Bimbisâra[1]; from east to west about five or six le, and from north to south seven or eight. It was here that Śâriputtra and Maudgalyâyana first saw Upasena[2]; that the Nirgrantha[3] made a pit of fire and poisoned the rice, and then invited Buddha (to eat with him); that king Ajâtaśatru made a black elephant intoxicated with liquor, wishing him to injure Buddha[4]; and that at the north-east corner of the city in a (large) curving (space) Jîvaka built a vihâra in the garden of Âmbapâlî[5], and invited Buddha with his 1250 disciples to it, that he might there make his offerings to support them. (These places) are still there as of old, but inside the city all is emptiness and desolation; no man dwells in it.

CHAPTER XXIX.

GṚIDHRA-KÛṬA HILL, AND LEGENDS. FÂ-HIEN PASSES A NIGHT ON IT. HIS REFLECTIONS.

ENTERING the valley, and keeping along the mountains on the south-east, after ascending fifteen le, (the travellers) came to mount Gṛidhra-

[1] See note 5, p. 81.

[2] One of the five first followers of Śâkyamuni. He is also called Aśvajit; in Pâli Assaji; but Aśvajit seems to be a military title='Master or trainer of horses.' The two more famous disciples met him, not to lead him, but to be directed by him, to Buddha. See Sacred Books of the East, vol. xiii, Vinaya Texts, pp. 144–147.

[3] One of the six Tîrthyas (Tîrthakas='erroneous teachers;' M. B., pp. 290–292, but I have not found the particulars of the attempts on Buddha's life referred to by Fâ-hien), or Brahmanical opponents of Buddha. He was an ascetic, one of the Jñâti clan, and is therefore called Nirgranthajñâti. He taught a system of fatalism, condemned the use of clothes, and thought he could subdue all passions by fasting. He had a body of followers, who called themselves by his name (Eitel, pp. 84, 85), and were the forerunners of the Jains.

[4] The king was moved to this by Devadatta. Of course the elephant disappointed them, and did homage to Śâkyamuni. See Sacred Books of the East, vol. xx, Vinaya Texts, p. 247.

[5] See note 3, p. 72. Jîvaka was Âmbapâlî's son by king Bimbisâra, and devoted himself to the practice of medicine. See the account of him in the Sacred Books of the East, vol. xvii, Vinaya Texts, pp. 171–194.

kûṭa[1]. Three le before you reach the top, there is a cavern in the rocks, facing the south, in which Buddha sat in meditation. Thirty paces to the north-west there is another, where Ânanda was sitting in meditation, when the deva Mâra Piśuna[2], having assumed the form of a large vulture, took his place in front of the cavern, and frightened the disciple. Then Buddha, by his mysterious, supernatural power, made a cleft in the rock, introduced his hand, and stroked Ânanda's shoulder, so that his fear immediately passed away. The footprints of the bird and the cleft for (Buddha's) hand are still there, and hence comes the name of 'The Hill of the Vulture Cavern.'

In front of the cavern there are the places where the four Buddhas sat. There are caverns also of the Arhats, one where each sat and meditated, amounting to several hundred in all. At the place where in front of his rocky apartment Buddha was walking from east to west (in meditation), and Devadatta, from among the beetling cliffs on the north of the mountain, threw a rock across, and hurt Buddha's toes[3], the rock is still there[4].

The hall where Buddha preached his Law has been destroyed, and only the foundations of the brick walls remain. On this hill the peak is beautifully green, and rises grandly up; it is the highest of all the five hills. In the New City Fâ-hien bought incense-(sticks), flowers, oil and lamps, and hired two bhikshus, long resident (at the place), to carry them (to the peak). When he himself got to it, he made his offerings with the flowers and incense, and lighted the lamps when the darkness began to come on. He felt melancholy, but restrained his tears and said, 'Here Buddha delivered the Śûrâṅgama (Sûtra)[5]. I, Fâ-hien, was born when I could not meet with Buddha; and now I only see the

---

[1] See note 4, p. 80.

[2] See note 4, p. 74. Piśuna is a name given to Mâra, and signifies 'sinful lust.'

[3] See M. B., p. 320. Hardy says that Devadatta's attempt was 'by the help of a machine;' but the oldest account in the Sacred Books of the East, vol. xx, Vinaya Texts, p. 245, agrees with what Fâ-hien implies that he threw the rock with his own arm.

[4] And, as described by Hsüan-chwang, fourteen or fifteen cubits high, and thirty paces round.

[5] See Mr. Bunyiu Nanjio's 'Catalogue of the Chinese Translation of the Buddhist

footprints which he has left, and the place where he lived, and nothing more.' With this, in front of the rock cavern, he chanted the Śûrâṅgama Sûtra, remained there over the night, and then returned towards the New City[1].

CHAPTER XXX.

THE ŚRATAPARṆA CAVE, OR CAVE OF THE FIRST COUNCIL. LEGENDS. SUICIDE OF A BHIKSHU.

OUT from the old city, after walking over 300 paces, on the west of the road, (the travellers) found the Karaṇḍa Bamboo garden[2], where the (old) vihâra is still in existence, with a company of monks, who keep (the ground about it) swept and watered.

North of the vihâra two or three le there was the Śmaśânam, which name means in Chinese 'the field of graves into which the dead are thrown[3].'

Tripiṭaka,' Sûtra Piṭaka, Nos. 399, 446. It was the former of these that came on this occasion to the thoughts and memory of Fâ-hien.

[1] In a note (p. lx) to his revised version of our author, Mr. Beal says, 'There is a full account of this perilous visit of Fâ-hien, and how he was attacked by tigers, in the "History of the High Priests."' But 'the high priests' merely means distinguished monks, 'eminent monks,' as Mr. Nanjio exactly renders the adjectival character. Nor was Fâ-hien 'attacked by tigers' on the peak. No 'tigers' appear in the Memoir. 'Two black lions' indeed crouched before him for a time this night, 'licking their lips and waving their tails;' but their appearance was to 'try,' and not to attack him; and when they saw him resolute, they 'drooped their heads, put down their tails, and prostrated themselves before him.' This of course is not an historical account, but a legendary tribute to his bold perseverance.

[2] Karaṇḍa Veṇuvana; a park presented to Buddha by king Bimbisâra, who also built a vihâra in it. See the account of the transaction in M. B., p. 194. The place was called Karaṇḍa, from a creature so named, which awoke the king just as a snake was about to bite him, and thus saved his life. In Hardy the creature appears as a squirrel, but Eitel says that the Karaṇḍa is a bird of a sweet voice, resembling a magpie, but herding in flocks; the cuculus melanoleucus. See 'Buddhist Birth Stories,' p. 118.

[3] The language here is rather contemptuous, as if our author had no sympathy

As they kept along the mountain on the south, and went west for 300 paces, they found a dwelling among the rocks, named the Pippala cave[1], in which Buddha regularly sat in meditation after taking his (midday) meal.

Going on still to the west for five or six le, on the north of the hill, in the shade, they found the cavern called Śrataparṇa[2], the place where, after the nirvâṇa[3] of Buddha, 500 Arhats collected the Sûtras. When they brought the Sûtras forth, three lofty seats[4] had been prepared and grandly ornamented. Śâriputtra occupied the one on the left, and Maudgalyâyana that on the right. Of the number of five hundred one was wanting. Mahâkaśyapa was president (on the middle seat). Ânanda was then outside the door, and could not get in[5]. At the place there was (subsequently) raised a tope, which is still existing.

Along (the sides of) the hill, there are also a very great many cells among the rocks, where the various Arhans sat and meditated. As you

---

with any other mode of disposing of the dead, but by his own Buddhistic method of cremation.

[1] The Chinese characters used for the name of this cavern serve also to name the pippala (peepul) tree, the ficus religiosa. They make us think that there was such a tree overshadowing the cave; but Fâ-hien would hardly have neglected to mention such a circumstance.

[2] A very great place in the annals of Buddhism. The Council in the Śrataparṇa cave did not come together fortuitously, but appears to have been convoked by the older members to settle the rules and doctrines of the order. The cave was prepared for the occasion by king Ajâtaśatru. From the expression about the 'bringing forth of the King,' it would seem that the Sûtras or some of them had been already committed to writing. May not the meaning of King (經) here be extended to the Vinaya rules, as well as the Sûtras, and mean 'the standards' of the system generally? See Davids' Manual, chapter ix, and Sacred Books of the East, vol. xx, Vinaya Texts, pp. 370–385.

[3] So in the text, evidently for pari-nirvâṇa.

[4] Instead of 'high' seats, the Chinese texts have 'vacant.' The character for 'prepared' denotes 'spread;'—they were carpeted; perhaps, both cushioned and carpeted, being rugs spread on the ground, raised higher than the other places for seats.

[5] Did they not contrive to let him in, with some cachinnation, even in so august an assembly, that so important a member should have been shut out?

leave the old city on the north, and go down east for three le, there is the rock dwelling of Devadatta, and at a distance of fifty paces from it there is a large, square, black rock. Formerly there was a bhikshu, who, as he walked backwards and forwards upon it, thought with himself:—'This body[1] is impermanent, a thing of bitterness and vanity[2], and which cannot be looked on as pure[3]. I am weary of this body, and troubled by it as an evil.' With this he grasped a knife, and was about to kill himself. But he thought again:—'The World-honoured one laid down a prohibition against one's killing himself[4].' Further it occurred to him:—'Yes, he did; but I now only wish to kill three poisonous thieves[5].' Immediately with the knife he cut his throat. With the first gash into the flesh he attained the state of a Śrotâpanna[6]; when he had gone half through, he attained to be an Anâgâmin[7]; and when he had cut right through, he was an Arhat, and attained to pari-nirvâṇa[8]; (and died).

---

[1] 'The life of this body' would, I think, fairly express the idea of the bhikshu.

[2] See the account of Buddha's preaching in chapter xviii.

[3] The sentiment of this clause is not easily caught.

[4] See E. M., p. 152:—'Buddha made a law forbidding the monks to commit suicide. He prohibited any one from discoursing on the miseries of life in such a manner as to cause desperation.' See also M. B., pp. 464, 465.

[5] Beal says:—'Evil desire; hatred; ignorance.'

[6] See note 2, p. 57.

[7] The Anâgâmin belong to the third degree of Buddhistic saintship, the third class of Âryas (note 2, page 57), who are no more liable to be reborn as men, but are to be born once more as devas, when they will forthwith become Arhats, and attain to nirvâṇa. E. H., pp. 8, 9.

[8] Our author expresses no opinion of his own on the act of this bhikshu. Must it not have been a good act, when it was attended, in the very act of performance, by such blessed consequences? But if Buddhism had not something better to show than what appears here, it would not attract the interest which it now does. The bhikshu was evidently rather out of his mind; and the verdict of a coroner's inquest of this nineteenth century would have pronounced that he killed himself 'in a fit of insanity.'

IV. BUDDHA IN SOLITUDE AND ENDURING AUSTERITIES. Ch. 31.

CHAPTER XXXI.

GAYÂ. ŚÂKYAMUNI'S ATTAINING TO THE BUDDHASHIP; AND OTHER LEGENDS.

FROM this place, after travelling to the west for four yojanas, (the pilgrims) came to the city of Gayâ[1]; but inside the city all was emptiness and desolation. Going on again to the south for twenty le, they arrived at the place where the Bodhisattva for six years practised with himself painful austerities. All around was forest.

Three le west from here they came to the place where, when Buddha had gone into the water to bathe, a deva bent down the branch of a tree, by means of which he succeeded in getting out of the pool[2].

Two le north from this was the place where the Grâmika girls presented to Buddha the rice-gruel made with milk[3]; and two le north from this (again) was the place where, seated on a rock under a great tree, and facing the east, he ate (the gruel). The tree and the rock are there at the present day. The rock may be six cubits in breadth and length, and rather more than two cubits in height. In Central India the cold and heat are so equally tempered that trees will live in it for several thousand and even for ten thousand years.

Half a yojana from this place to the north-east there was a cavern in

---

[1] Gayâ, a city of Magadha, was north-west of the present Gayah (lat. 24° 47′ N., lon. 85° 1′ E.). It was here that Śâkyamuni lived for seven years, after quitting his family, until he attained to Buddhaship. The place is still frequented by pilgrims. E. H., p. 41.

[2] This is told so as to make us think that he was in danger of being drowned; but this does not appear in the only other account of the incident I have met with,—in 'The Life of the Buddha,' p. 31. And he was not yet Buddha, though he is here called so; unless indeed the narrative is confused, and the incidents do not follow in the order of time.

[3] An incident similar to this is told, with many additions, in Hardy's M. B., pp. 166–168; 'The Life of the Buddha,' p. 30; and the 'Buddhist Birth Stories,' pp. 91, 92; but the name of the ministering girl or girls is different. I take Grâmika from a note in Beal's revised version; it seems to me a happy solution of the difficulty caused by the 彌家 of Fâ-hien.

the rocks, into which the Bodhisattva entered, and sat cross-legged with his face to the west. (As he did so), he said to himself, 'If I am to attain to perfect wisdom (and become Buddha), let there be a supernatural attestation of it.' On the wall of the rock there appeared immediately the shadow of a Buddha, rather more than three feet in length, which is still bright at the present day. At this moment heaven and earth were greatly moved, and devas in the air spoke plainly, 'This is not the place where any Buddha of the past, or he that is to come, has attained, or will attain, to perfect Wisdom. Less than half a yojana from this to the south-west will bring you to the patra[1] tree, where all past Buddhas have attained, and all to come must attain, to perfect Wisdom.' When they had spoken these words, they immediately led the way forwards to the place, singing as they did so. As they thus went away, the Bodhisattva arose and walked (after them). At a distance of thirty paces from the tree, a deva gave him the grass of lucky omen[2], which he received and went on. After (he had proceeded) fifteen paces, 500 green birds came flying towards him, went round him thrice, and disappeared. The Bodhisattva went forward to the patra tree, placed the kuśa grass at the foot of it, and sat down with his face to the east. Then king Mâra sent three beautiful young ladies, who came from the north, to tempt him, while he himself came from the south to do the same. The Bodhisattva put his toes down on the ground, and the demon soldiers retired and dispersed, and the three young ladies were changed into old (grand-) mothers[3].

At the place mentioned above of the six years' painful austerities, and at all these other places, men subsequently reared topes and set up images, which all exist at the present day.

Where Buddha, after attaining to perfect wisdom, for seven days contemplated the tree, and experienced the joy of vimukti[4]; where, under

---

[1] Called 'the tree of leaves,' and 'the tree of reflection;' a palm tree, the borassus flabellifera, described as a tree which never loses its leaves. It is often confounded with the pippala. E. H., p. 92.

[2] The kuśa grass, mentioned in a previous note.

[3] See the account of this contest with Mâra in M. B., pp. 171–179, and 'Buddhist Birth Stories,' pp. 96–101.

[4] See note 2, p. 38.

V. BUDDHASHIP ATTAINED. Ch. 31.

the patra tree, he walked backwards and forwards from west to east for seven days; where the devas made a hall appear, composed of the seven precious substances, and presented offerings to him for seven days; where the blind dragon Muchilinda[1] encircled him for seven days; where he sat under the nyagrodha tree, on a square rock, with his face to the east, and Brahma-deva[2] came and made his request to him; where the four deva kings brought to him their alms-bowls[3]; where the 500 merchants[4] presented to him the roasted flour and honey; and where he converted the brothers Kaśyapa and their thousand disciples[5];—at all these places topes were reared.

At the place where Buddha attained to perfect Wisdom, there are three monasteries, in all of which there are monks residing. The families of their people around supply the societies of these monks with an abundant sufficiency of what they require, so that there is no lack or stint[6]. The disciplinary rules are strictly observed by them. The laws regulating their demeanour in sitting, rising, and entering when the others are assembled, are those which have been practised by all the saints since

---

[1] Called also Mahâ, or the Great Muchilinda. Eitel says: 'A nâga king, the tutelary deity of a lake near which Śâkyamuni once sat for seven days absorbed in meditation, whilst the king guarded him.' The account (p. 35) in 'The Life of the Buddha' is:—'Buddha went to where lived the nâga king Muchilinda, and he, wishing to preserve him from the sun and rain, wrapped his body seven times round him, and spread out his hood over his head; and there he remained seven days in thought.' So also the Nidâna Kathâ, in 'Buddhist Birth Stories,' p. 109.

[2] This was Brahmâ himself, though 'king' is omitted. What he requested of the Buddha was that he would begin the preaching of his Law. Nidâna Kathâ, p. 111.

[3] See note 4, p. 35.

[4] The other accounts mention only two; but in M. B., p. 182, and the Nidâna Kathâ, p. 110, these two have 500 well-laden waggons with them.

[5] These must not be confounded with Mahâkaśyapa of note 5, p. 45. They were three brothers, Uruvilvâ, Gayâ, and Nadî-Kaśyapa, up to this time holders of 'erroneous' views, having 500, 300, and 200 disciples respectively. They became distinguished followers of Śâkyamuni; and are—each of them—to become Buddha by-and-by. See the Nidâna Kathâ, pp. 114, 115.

[6] This seems to be the meaning; but I do not wonder that some understand the sentence of the benevolence of the monkish population to the travellers.

Buddha was in the world down to the present day. The places of the four great topes have been fixed, and handed down without break, since Buddha attained to nirvâṇa. Those four great topes are those at the places where Buddha was born; where he attained to Wisdom; where he (began to) move the wheel of his Law; and where he attained to pari-nirvâṇa.

CHAPTER XXXII.

LEGEND OF KING AŚOKA IN A FORMER BIRTH, AND HIS NARAKA.

WHEN king Aśoka, in a former birth[1], was a little boy and playing on the road, he met Kaśyapa Buddha walking. (The stranger) begged food, and the boy pleasantly took a handful of earth and gave it to him. The Buddha took the earth, and returned it to the ground on which he was walking; but because of this (the boy) received the recompense of becoming a king of the iron wheel[2], to rule over Jambudvîpa. (Once) when he was making a judicial tour of inspection through Jambudvîpa, he saw, between the iron circuit of the two hills, a naraka[3] for the punishment of wicked men. Having thereupon asked his ministers what sort of a thing it was, they replied, 'It belongs to Yama[4], king of

[1] Here is an instance of 昔 used, as was pointed out in note 3, page 30, for a former age; and not merely a former time. Perhaps 'a former birth' is the best translation. The Corean reading of Kaśyapa Buddha is certainly preferable to the Chinese 'Śâkya Buddha.'

[2] See note 3, p. 49.

[3] I prefer to retain the Sanskrit term here, instead of translating the Chinese text by 'Earth's prison (地 獄),' or 'a prison in the earth;' the name which has been adopted generally by Christian missionaries in China for gehenna and hell.

[4] Eitel (p. 173) says:—'Yama was originally the Âryan god of the dead, living in a heaven above the world, the regent of the south; but Brahmanism transferred his abode to hell. Both views have been retained by Buddhism.' The Yama of the text is the 'regent of the narakas, residing south of Jambudvîpa, outside the Chakravâlas (the double circuit of mountains above), in a palace built of brass and iron. He has a sister who controls all the female culprits, as

demons, for punishing wicked people.' The king thought within himself:—'(Even) the king of demons is able to make a naraka in which to deal with wicked men; why should not I, who am the lord of men, make a naraka in which to deal with wicked men?' He forthwith asked his ministers who could make for him a naraka and preside over the punishment of wicked people in it. They replied that it was only a man of extreme wickedness who could make it; and the king thereupon sent officers to seek everywhere for (such) a bad man; and they saw by the side of a pond a man tall and strong, with a black countenance, yellow hair, and green eyes, hooking up the fish with his feet, while he called to him birds and beasts, and, when they came, then shot and killed them, so that not one escaped. Having got this man, they took him to the king, who secretly charged him, 'You must make a square enclosure with high walls. Plant in it all kinds of flowers and fruits; make good ponds in it for bathing; make it grand and imposing in every way, so that men shall look to it with thirsting desire; make its gates strong and sure; and when any one enters, instantly seize him and punish him as a sinner, not allowing him to get out. Even if I should enter, punish me as a sinner in the same way, and do not let me go. I now appoint you master of that naraka.'

Soon after this a bhikshu, pursuing his regular course of begging his food, entered the gate (of the place). When the lictors of the naraka saw him, they were about to subject him to their tortures; but he, frightened, begged them to allow him a moment in which to eat his midday meal. Immediately after, there came in another man, whom they thrust into a mortar and pounded till a red froth overflowed. As the bhikshu looked on, there came to him the thought of the impermanence, the painful suffering and inanity of this body, and how it is but as a bubble and as foam; and instantly he attained to Arhatship. Immediately after, the lictors seized him, and threw him into a caldron of

he exclusively deals with the male sex. Three times, however, in every twenty-four hours, a demon pours boiling copper into Yama's mouth, and squeezes it down his throat, causing him unspeakable pain.' Such, however, is the wonderful 'transrotation of births,' that when Yama's sins have been expiated, he is to be reborn as Buddha, under the name of 'The Universal King.'

boiling water. There was a look of joyful satisfaction, however, in the bhikshu's countenance. The fire was extinguished, and the water became cold. In the middle (of the caldron) there rose up a lotus flower, with the bhikshu seated on it. The lictors at once went and reported to the king that there was a marvellous occurrence in the naraka, and wished him to go and see it; but the king said, 'I formerly made such an agreement that now I dare not go (to the place).' The lictors said, 'This is not a small matter. Your majesty ought to go quickly. Let your former agreement be altered.' The king thereupon followed them, and entered (the naraka), when the bhikshu preached the Law to him, and he believed, and was made free[1]. Forthwith he demolished the naraka, and repented of all the evil which he had formerly done. From this time he believed in and honoured the Three Precious Ones, and constantly went to a patra tree, repenting under it, with self-reproach, of his errors, and accepting the eight rules of abstinence[2].

The queen asked where the king was constantly going to, and the ministers replied that he was constantly to be seen under (such and such) a patra tree. She watched for a time when the king was not there, and then sent men to cut the tree down. When the king came, and saw what had been done, he swooned away with sorrow, and fell to the ground. His ministers sprinkled water on his face, and after a considerable time he revived. He then built all round (the stump) with bricks, and poured a hundred pitchers of cows' milk on the roots; and as he lay with his four limbs spread out on the ground, he took this oath, 'If the tree do not live, I will never rise from this.' When he had uttered this oath, the tree immediately began to grow from the roots, and it has continued to grow till now, when it is nearly 100 cubits in height.

CHAPTER XXXIII.

MOUNT GURUPADA, WHERE KAŚYAPA BUDDHA'S ENTIRE SKELETON IS.

(THE travellers), going on from this three le to the south, came to a mountain named Gurupada[3], inside which Mahâkaśyapa even

---

[1] Or, 'was loosed;' from the bonds, I suppose, of his various illusions.

[2] I have not met with this particular numerical category.

[3] 'Fowl's-foot hill,' 'with three peaks, resembling the foot of a chicken. It lies

now is. He made a cleft, and went down into it, though the place where he entered would not (now) admit a man. Having gone down very far, there was a hole on one side, and there the complete body of Kaśyapa (still) abides. Outside the hole (at which he entered) is the earth with which he had washed his hands[1]. If the people living thereabouts have a sore on their heads, they plaster on it some of the earth from this, and feel immediately easier[2]. On this mountain, now as of old, there are Arhats abiding. Devotees of our Law from the various countries in that quarter go year by year to the mountain, and present offerings to Kaśyapa; and to those whose hearts are strong in faith there come Arhats at night, and talk with them, discussing and explaining their doubts, and disappearing suddenly afterwards.

On this hill hazels grow luxuriantly; and there are many lions, tigers, and wolves, so that people should not travel incautiously.

CHAPTER XXXIV.

ON THE WAY BACK TO PATNA. VÂRÂṆASÎ, OR BENÂRES. ŚÂKYAMUNI'S FIRST DOINGS AFTER BECOMING BUDDHA.

FÂ-HIEN[3] returned (from here) towards Pâṭaliputtra[4], keeping along the course of the Ganges and descending in the direction of the west.

---

seven miles south-east of Gayâ, and was the residence of Mahâkaśyapa, who is said to be still living inside this mountain.' So Eitel says, p. 58; but this chapter does not say that Kaśyapa is in the mountain alive, but that his body entire is in a recess or hole in it. Hardy (M. B., p. 97) says that after Kaśyapa Buddha's body was burnt, the bones still remained in their usual position, presenting the appearance of a perfect skeleton. It is of him that the chapter speaks, and not of the famous disciple of Śâkyamuni, who also is called Mahâkaśyapa. This will appear also on a comparison of Eitel's articles on 'Mahâkaśyapa' and 'Kaśyapa Buddha.'

[1] Was it a custom to wash the hands with 'earth,' as is often done with sand?

[2] This I conceive to be the meaning here.

[3] Fâ-hien is here mentioned singly, as in the account of his visit to the cave on Gṛidhra-kûṭa. I think that Tâo-ching may have remained at Patna after their first visit to it.

[4] See note 1, p. 77.

After going ten yojanas he found a vihâra, named 'The Wilderness,'—a place where Buddha had dwelt, and where there are monks now.

Pursuing the same course, and going still to the west, he arrived, after twelve yojanas, at the city of Vârâṇasî[1] in the kingdom of Kâśî. Rather more than ten le to the north-east of the city, he found the vihâra in the park of 'The ṛishi's Deer-wild[2].' In this park there formerly resided a Pratyeka Buddha[3], with whom the deer were regularly in the habit of stopping for the night. When the World-honoured one was about to attain to perfect Wisdom, the devas sang in the sky, 'The son of king Śuddhodana, having quitted his family and studied the Path (of Wisdom)[4], will now in seven days become Buddha.' The Pratyeka Buddha heard their words, and immediately attained to nirvâṇa; and hence this place was named 'The Park of the ṛishi's Deer-wild[5].' After the World-honoured one had attained to perfect Wisdom, men built the vihâra in it.

Buddha wished to convert Kauṇḍinya[6] and his four companions; but

---

[1] 'The city surrounded by rivers;' the modern Benâres, lat. 25° 23′ N., lon. 83° 5′ E.

[2] 'The ṛishi,' says Eitel, 'is a man whose bodily frame has undergone a certain transformation by dint of meditation and asceticism, so that he is, for an indefinite period, exempt from decrepitude, age, and death. As this period is believed to extend far beyond the usual duration of human life, such persons are called, and popularly believed to be, immortals' Ṛishis are divided into various classes; and ṛishi-ism is spoken of as a seventh path of transrotation, and ṛishis are referred to as the seventh class of sentient beings. Tâoism, as well as Buddhism, has its Seen jin.

[3] See note 2, p. 40.

[4] See note 4, p. 64.

[5] For another legend about this park, and the identification with 'a fine wood' still existing, see note in Beal's first version, p. 135.

[6] A prince of Magadha and a maternal uncle of Śâkyamuni, who gave him the name of Ajñâta, meaning automat; and hence he often appears as Ajñâta Kauṇḍinya. He and his four friends had followed Śâkyamuni into the Uruvilvâ desert, sympathising with him in the austerities he endured, and hoping that they would issue in his Buddhaship. They were not aware that that issue had come; which may show us that all the accounts in the thirty-first chapter

they, (being aware of his intention), said to one another, 'This Śramaṇa Gotama[1] for six years continued in the practice of painful austerities, eating daily (only) a single hemp-seed, and one grain of rice, without attaining to the Path (of Wisdom); how much less will he do so now that he has entered (again) among men, and is giving the reins to (the indulgence of) his body, his speech, and his thoughts! What has he to do with the Path (of Wisdom)? To-day, when he comes to us, let us be on our guard not to speak with him.' At the places where the five men all rose up, and respectfully saluted (Buddha), when he came to them; where, sixty paces north from this, he sat with his face to the east, and first turned the wheel of the Law, converting Kauṇḍinya and the four others; where,

---

are merely descriptions, by means of external imagery, of what had taken place internally. The kingdom of nirvâṇa had come without observation. These friends knew it not; and they were offended by what they considered Śâkyamuni's failure, and the course he was now pursuing. See the account of their conversion in M. B., p. 186.

[1] This is the only instance in Fâ-hien's text where the Bodhisattva or Buddha is called by the surname 'Gotama.' For the most part our traveller uses Buddha as a proper name, though it properly means 'The Enlightened.' He uses also the combinations 'Śâkya Buddha,'='The Buddha of the Śâkya tribe,' and 'Śâkyamuni,'='The Śâkya sage.' This last is the most common designation of the Buddha in China, and to my mind best combines the characteristics of a descriptive and a proper name. Among other Buddhistic peoples 'Gotama' and 'Gotama Buddha' are the more frequent designations. It is not easy to account for the rise of the surname Gotama in the Śâkya family, as Oldenberg acknowledges. He says that 'the Śâkyas, in accordance with the custom of Indian noble families, had borrowed it from one of the ancient Vedic bard families.' Dr. Davids ('Buddhism,' p. 27) says: 'The family name was certainly Gautama,' adding in a note, 'It is a curious fact that Gautama is still the family name of the Rajput chiefs of Nagara, the village which has been identified with Kapilavastu.' Dr. Eitel says that 'Gautama was the sacerdotal name of the Śâkya family, which counted the ancient ṛishi Gautama among its ancestors.' When we proceed, however, to endeavour to trace the connexion of that Brahmanical ṛishi with the Śâkya house, by means of 1323, 1468, 1469, and other historical works in Nanjio's Catalogue, we soon find that Indian histories have no surer foundation than the shifting sand;—see E. H., on the name Śâkya, pp. 108, 109. We must be content for the present simply to accept Gotama as one of the surnames of the Buddha with whom we have to do.

twenty paces further to the north, he delivered his prophecy concerning Maitreya[1]; and where, at a distance of fifty paces to the south, the dragon Elâpattra[2] asked him, 'When shall I get free from this nâga body?'—at all these places topes were reared, and are still existing. In (the park) there are two monasteries, in both of which there are monks residing.

When you go north-west from the vihâra of the Deer-wild park for thirteen yojanas, there is a kingdom named Kauśâmbî[3]. Its vihâra is named Ghochiravana[4]—a place where Buddha formerly resided. Now, as of old, there is a company of monks there, most of whom are students of the hînayâna.

East from (this), when you have travelled eight yojanas, is the place where Buddha converted[5] the evil demon. There, and where he walked (in meditation) and sat at the place which was his regular abode, there have been topes erected. There is also a monastery, which may contain more than a hundred monks.

CHAPTER XXXV.

DAKSHIṆA, AND THE PIGEON MONASTERY.

SOUTH from this 200 yojanas, there is a country named Dakshiṇa[6], where there is a monastery (dedicated to) the bygone Kaśyapa Buddha,

---

[1] See note 3, p. 25. It is there said that the prediction of Maitreya's succession to the Buddhaship was made to him in the Tushita heaven. Was there a repetition of it here in the Deer-park, or was a prediction now given concerning something else?

[2] Nothing seems to be known of this nâga but what we read here.

[3] Identified by some with Kusia, near Kurrah (lat. 25° 41′ N., lon. 81° 27′ E.); by others with Kosam on the Jumna, thirty miles above Allahabad. See E. H., p. 55.

[4] Ghochira was the name of a Vaiśya elder, or head, who presented a garden and vihâra to Buddha. Hardy (M. B., p. 356) quotes a statement from a Singhalese authority that Śâkyamuni resided here during the ninth year of his Buddhaship.

[5] Dr. Davids thinks this may refer to the striking and beautiful story of the conversion of the Yakkha Âḷavaka, as related in the Uragavagga, Âḷavakasutta, pp. 29–31 (Sacred Books of the East, vol. x, part ii).

[6] Said to be the ancient name for the Deccan. As to the various marvels in the chapter, it must be borne in mind that our author, as he tells us at the end, only gives them from hearsay. See 'Buddhist Records of the Western World,' vol. ii, pp. 214, 215, where the description, however, is very different.

and which has been hewn out from a large hill of rock. It consists in all of five storeys;—the lowest, having the form of an elephant, with 500 apartments in the rock; the second, having the form of a lion, with 400 apartments; the third, having the form of a horse, with 300 apartments; the fourth, having the form of an ox, with 200 apartments; and the fifth, having the form of a pigeon, with 100 apartments. At the very top there is a spring, the water of which, always in front of the apartments in the rock, goes round among the rooms, now circling, now curving, till in this way it arrives at the lowest storey, having followed the shape of the structure, and flows out there at the door. Everywhere in the apartments of the monks, the rock has been pierced so as to form windows for the admission of light, so that they are all bright, without any being left in darkness. At the four corners of the (tiers of) apartments, the rock has been hewn so as to form steps for ascending to the top (of each). The men of the present day, being of small size, and going up step by step, manage to get to the top; but in a former age they did so at one step[1]. Because of this, the monastery is called Paravata, that being the Indian name for a pigeon. There are always Arhats residing in it.

The country about is (a tract of) uncultivated hillocks[2], without inhabitants. At a very long distance from the hill there are villages, where the people all have bad and erroneous views, and do not know the Śramaṇas of the Law of Buddha, Brâhmaṇas, or (devotees of) any of the other and different schools. The people of that country are constantly seeing men on the wing, who come and enter this monastery. On one occasion, when devotees of various countries came to perform their worship at it, the people of those villages said to them, 'Why do you not fly? The devotees whom we have seen hereabouts all fly;' and the strangers answered, on the spur of the moment, 'Our wings are not yet fully formed.'

The kingdom of Dakshiṇa is out of the way, and perilous to traverse. There are difficulties in connexion with the roads; but those who know

---

[1] Compare the account of Buddha's great stride of fifteen yojanas in Ceylon, as related in chapter xxxviii.

[2] See the same phrase in the Books of the Later Han dynasty, the twenty-fourth Book of Biographies, p. 9 b.

how to manage such difficulties and wish to proceed should bring with them money and various articles, and give them to the king. He will then send men to escort them. These will (at different stages) pass them over to others, who will show them the shortest routes. Fâ-hien, however, was after all unable to go there; but having received the (above) accounts from men of the country, he has narrated them.

CHAPTER XXXVI.

IN PATNA. FÂ-HIEN'S LABOURS IN TRANSCRIPTION OF MANUSCRIPTS, AND INDIAN STUDIES FOR THREE YEARS.

FROM Vârâṇasî (the travellers) went back east to Pâṭaliputtra. Fâ-hien's original object had been to search for (copies of) the Vinaya. In the various kingdoms of North India, however, he had found one master transmitting orally (the rules) to another, but no written copies which he could transcribe. He had therefore travelled far and come on to Central India. Here, in the mahâyâna monastery[1], he found a copy of the Vinaya, containing the Mahâsâṅghika[2] rules,—those which were observed in the first Great Council, while Buddha was still in the world. The original copy was handed down in the Jetavana vihâra. As to the other eighteen schools[3], each one has the views and decisions of its own masters.

---

[1] Mentioned before in chapter xxvii.

[2] Mahâsâṅghikâḥ simply means 'the Great Assembly,' that is, of monks. When was this first assembly in the time of Śâkyamuni held? It does not appear that the rules observed at it were written down at the time. The document found by Fâ-hien would be a record of those rules; or rather a copy of that record. We must suppose that the original record had disappeared from the Jetavana vihâra, or Fâ-hien would probably have spoken of it when he was there, and copied it, if he had been allowed to do so.

[3] The eighteen pû (部). Four times in this chapter the character called pû occurs, and in the first and two last instances it can only have the meaning, often belonging to it, of 'copy.' The second instance, however, is different. How should there be eighteen copies, all different from the original, and from one another, in minor matters? We are compelled to translate—'the eighteen schools,'

Those agree (with this) in the general meaning, but they have small and trivial differences, as when one opens and another shuts[1]. This copy (of the rules), however, is the most complete, with the fullest explanations[2].

He further got a transcript of the rules in six or seven thousand gâthas[3], being the sarvâstivâdâḥ[4] rules,—those which are observed by the communities of monks in the land of Ts'in; which also have all been handed down orally from master to master without being committed to writing. In the community here, moreover, he got the Saṃyuktâbhidharma-hṛidaya-(śâstra)[5], containing about six or seven thousand gâthas; he also got a Sûtra of 2500 gâthas; one chapter of the Parinirvâṇa-vaipulya Sûtra[6], of about 5000 gâthas; and the Mahâsâṅghikâḥ Abhidharma.

In consequence (of this success in his quest) Fâ-hien stayed here for three years, learning Sanskrit books and the Sanskrit speech, and writing out the Vinaya rules. When Tâo-ching arrived in the Central Kingdom, and saw the rules observed by the Śramaṇas, and the dignified demeanour in their societies which he remarked under all occurring circumstances, he sadly called to mind in what a mutilated and imperfect condition the rules were among the monkish communities in the land of Ts'in, and made the following aspiration:—'From this time forth till I come to the

---

an expression well known in all Buddhist writings. See Rhys Davids' Manual, p. 218, and the authorities there quoted.

[1] This is equivalent to the 'binding' and 'loosing,' 'opening' and 'shutting,' which found their way into the New Testament, and the Christian Church, from the schools of the Jewish Rabbins.

[2] It was afterwards translated by Fâ-hien into Chinese. See Nanjio's Catalogue of the Chinese Tripiṭaka, columns 400 and 401, and Nos. 1119 and 1150, columns 247 and 253.

[3] A gâthâ is a stanza, generally consisting, it has seemed to me, of a few, commonly of two, lines somewhat metrically arranged; but I do not know that its length is strictly defined.

[4] 'A branch,' says Eitel, 'of the great vaibhâshika school, asserting the reality of all visible phenomena, and claiming the authority of Râhula.'

[5] See Nanjio's Catalogue, No. 1287. He does not mention it in his account of Fâ-hien, who, he says, translated the Saṃyukta-piṭaka Sûtra.

[6] Probably Nanjio's Catalogue, No. 120; at any rate, connected with it.

state of Buddha, let me not be born in a frontier land[1].' He remained accordingly (in India), and did not return (to the land of Han). Fâ-hien, however, whose original purpose had been to secure the introduction of the complete Vinaya rules into the land of Han, returned there alone.

CHAPTER XXXVII.

TO CHAMPÂ AND TÂMALIPTÎ. STAY AND LABOURS THERE FOR THREE YEARS. TAKES SHIP TO SINGHALA, OR CEYLON.

FOLLOWING the course of the Ganges, and descending eastwards for eighteen yojanas, he found on the southern bank the great kingdom of Champâ[2], with topes reared at the places where Buddha walked in meditation by his vihâra, and where he and the three Buddhas, his predecessors, sat. There were monks residing at them all. Continuing his journey east for nearly fifty yojanas, he came to the country of Tâmaliptî[3], (the capital of which is) a seaport. In the country there are twenty-two monasteries, at all of which there are monks residing. The Law of Buddha is also flourishing in it. Here Fâ-hien stayed two years, writing out his Sûtras[4], and drawing pictures of images.

After this he embarked in a large merchant-vessel, and went floating over the sea to the south-west. It was the beginning of winter, and the wind was favourable; and, after fourteen days, sailing day and night, they came to the country of Singhala[5]. The people said that it was distant (from Tâmaliptî) about 700 yojanas.

---

[1] This then would be the consummation of the Śramaṇa's being,—to get to be Buddha, the Buddha of his time in his Kalpa; and Tâo-ching thought that he could attain to this consummation by a succession of births; and was likely to attain to it sooner by living only in India. If all this was not in his mind, he yet felt that each of his successive lives would be happier, if lived in India.

[2] Probably the modern Champanagur, three miles west of Baglipoor, lat. 25° 14′ N., lon. 56° 55′ E.

[3] Then the principal emporium for the trade with Ceylon and China; the modern Tam-look, lat. 22° 17′ N., lon. 88° 2′ E.; near the mouth of the Hoogly.

[4] Perhaps Ching (經) is used here for any portions of the Tripiṭaka which he had obtained.

[5] 'The Kingdom of the Lion,' Ceylon. Singhala was the name of a

The kingdom is on a large island, extending from east to west fifty yojanas, and from north to south thirty. Left and right from it there are as many as 100 small islands, distant from one another ten, twenty, or even 200 le; but all subject to the large island. Most of them produce pearls and precious stones of various kinds; there is one which produces the pure and brilliant pearl [1],—an island which would form a square of about ten le. The king employs men to watch and protect it, and requires three out of every ten such pearls, which the collectors find.

CHAPTER XXXVIII.

AT CEYLON. RISE OF THE KINGDOM. FEATS OF BUDDHA. TOPES AND MONASTERIES. STATUE OF BUDDHA IN JADE. BO TREE. FESTIVAL OF BUDDHA'S TOOTH.

THE country originally had no human inhabitants [2], but was occupied only by spirits and nâgas, with which merchants of various countries carried on a trade. When the trafficking was taking place, the spirits did not show themselves. They simply set forth their precious commodities, with labels of the price attached to them; while the merchants made their purchases according to the price; and took the things away.

Through the coming and going of the merchants (in this way), when they went away, the people of (their) various countries heard how pleasant the land was, and flocked to it in numbers till it became a

---

merchant adventurer from India, to whom the founding of the kingdom was ascribed. His father was named Singha, 'the Lion,' which became the name of the country;—Singhala, or Singha-Kingdom, 'the Country of the Lion.'

[1] Called the maṇi pearl or bead. Maṇi is explained as meaning 'free from stain,' 'bright and growing purer.' It is a symbol of Buddha and of his Law. The most valuable rosaries are made of maṇis.

[2] It is desirable to translate 人民, for which 'inhabitants' or 'people' is elsewhere sufficient, here by 'human inhabitants.' According to other accounts Singhala was originally occupied by Râkshasas or Rakshas, 'demons who devour men,' and 'beings to be feared,' monstrous cannibals or anthropophagi, the terror of the shipwrecked mariner. Our author's 'spirits' (鬼神) were of a gentler type. His dragons or nâgas have come before us again and again.

great nation. The (climate) is temperate and attractive, without any difference of summer and winter. The vegetation is always luxuriant. Cultivation proceeds whenever men think fit: there are no fixed seasons for it.

When Buddha came to this country[1], wishing to transform the wicked nâgas, by his supernatural power he planted one foot at the north of the royal city, and the other on the top of a mountain[2], the two being fifteen yojanas apart. Over the footprint at the north of the city the king built a large tope, 400 cubits high, grandly adorned with gold and silver, and finished with a combination of all the precious substances. By the side of the tope he further built a monastery, called the Abhayagiri[3], where there are (now) five thousand monks. There is in it a hall of Buddha, adorned with carved and inlaid work of gold and silver, and rich in the seven precious substances, in which there is an image (of Buddha) in green jade, more than twenty cubits in height, glittering all over with those substances, and having an appearance of solemn dignity which words cannot express. In the palm of the right hand there is a priceless pearl. Several years had now elapsed since Fâ-hien left the land of Han; the

---

[1] That Śâkyamuni ever visited Ceylon is to me more than doubtful. Hardy, in M. B., pp. 207–213, has brought together the legends of three visits,—in the first, fifth, and eighth years of his Buddhaship. It is plain, however, from Fâ-hien's narrative, that in the beginning of our fifth century, Buddhism prevailed throughout the island. Davids in the last chapter of his 'Buddhism' ascribes its introduction to one of Aśoka's missions, after the Council of Patna, under his son Mahinda, when Tissa, 'the delight of the gods,' was king (B. C. 250–230).

[2] This would be what is known as 'Adam's peak,' having, according to Hardy (pp. 211, 212, notes), the three names of Selesumano, Samastakûta, and Samanila. 'There is an indentation on the top of it,' a superficial hollow, 5 feet $3\frac{3}{4}$ inches long, and about $2\frac{1}{2}$ feet wide. The Hindus regard it as the footprint of Śiva; the Mohammedans, as that of Adam; and the Buddhists, as in the text,—as having been made by Buddha.

[3] Meaning 'The Fearless Hill.' There is still the Abhayagiri tope, the highest in Ceylon, according to Davids, 250 feet in height, and built about B. C. 90, by Waṭṭa Gâmiṇi, in whose reign, about 160 years after the Council of Patna, and 330 years after the death of Śâkyamuni, the Tripiṭaka was first reduced to writing in Ceylon;—'Buddhism,' p. 234.

men with whom he had been in intercourse had all been of regions strange to him; his eyes had not rested on an old and familiar hill or river, plant or tree: his fellow-travellers, moreover, had been separated from him, some by death, and others flowing off in different directions; no face or shadow was now with him but his own, and a constant sadness was in his heart. Suddenly (one day), when by the side of this image of jade, he saw a merchant presenting as his offering a fan of white silk[1]; and the tears of sorrow involuntarily filled his eyes and fell down.

A former king of the country had sent to Central India and got a slip of the patra tree[2], which he planted by the side of the hall of Buddha, where a tree grew up to the height of about 200 cubits. As it bent on one side towards the south-east, the king, fearing it would fall, propped it with a post eight or nine spans round. The tree began to grow at the very heart of the prop, where it met (the trunk); (a shoot) pierced through the post, and went down to the ground, where it entered and formed roots, that rose (to the surface) and were about four spans round. Although the post was split in the middle, the outer portions kept

---

[1] We naturally suppose that the merchant-offerer was a Chinese, as indeed the Chinese texts say, and the fan such as Fâ-hien had seen and used in his native land.

[2] This should be the pippala, or bodhidruma, generally spoken of, in connexion with Buddha, as the Bo tree, under which he attained to the Buddhaship. It is strange our author should have confounded them as he seems to do. In what we are told of the tree here, we have, no doubt, his account of the planting, growth, and preservation of the famous Bo tree, which still exists in Ceylon. It has been stated in a previous note that Aśoka's son, Mahinda, went as the apostle of Buddhism to Ceylon. By-and-by he sent for his sister Sanghamittâ, who had entered the order at the same time as himself, and whose help was needed, some of the king's female relations having signified their wish to become nuns. On leaving India, she took with her a branch of the sacred Bo tree at Buddha Gayâ, under which Śâkyamuni had become Buddha. Of how the tree has grown and still lives we have an account in Davids' 'Buddhism.' He quotes the words of Sir Emerson Tennent, that it is 'the oldest historical tree in the world;' but this must be denied if it be true, as Eitel says, that the tree at Buddha Gayâ, from which the slip that grew to be this tree was taken more than 2000 years ago, is itself still living in its place. We might conclude that Fâ-hien, when in Ceylon, heard neither of Mahinda nor Sanghamittâ.

hold (of the shoot), and people did not remove them. Beneath the tree there has been built a vihâra, in which there is an image (of Buddha) seated, which the monks and commonalty reverence and look up to without ever becoming wearied. In the city there has been reared also the vihâra of Buddha's tooth, on which, as well as on the other, the seven precious substances have been employed.

The king practises the Brahmanical purifications, and the sincerity of the faith and reverence of the population inside the city are also great. Since the establishment of government in the kingdom there has been no famine or scarcity, no revolution or disorder. In the treasuries of the monkish communities there are many precious stones, and the priceless maṇis. One of the kings (once) entered one of those treasuries, and when he looked all round and saw the priceless pearls, his covetous greed was excited, and he wished to take them to himself by force. In three days, however, he came to himself, and immediately went and bowed his head to the ground in the midst of the monks, to show his repentance of the evil thought. As a sequel to this, he informed the monks (of what had been in his mind), and desired them to make a regulation that from that day forth the king should not be allowed to enter the treasury and see (what it contained), and that no bhikshu should enter it till after he had been in orders for a period of full forty years [1].

In the city there are many Vaiśya elders and Sabæan [2] merchants, whose houses are stately and beautiful. The lanes and passages are kept in good order. At the heads of the four principal streets there have been built preaching halls, where, on the eighth, fourteenth, and fifteenth days of the month, they spread carpets, and set forth a pulpit, while the monks and commonalty from all quarters come together to hear the Law. The people say that in the kingdom there may be altogether sixty thousand monks, who get their food from their common stores.

[1] Compare what is said in chap. xvi, about the inquiries made at monasteries as to the standing of visitors in the monkhood, and duration of their ministry.

[2] The phonetic values of the two Chinese characters here are in Sanskrit sâ; and vâ, bo or bhâ. 'Sabæan' is Mr. Beal's reading of them, probably correct. I suppose the merchants were Arabs, forerunners of the so-called Moormen, who still form so important a part of the mercantile community in Ceylon.

The king, besides, prepares elsewhere in the city a common supply of food for five or six thousand more. When any want, they take their great bowls, and go (to the place of distribution), and take as much as the vessels will hold, all returning with them full.

The tooth of Buddha is always brought forth in the middle of the third month. Ten days beforehand the king grandly caparisons a large elephant, on which he mounts a man who can speak distinctly, and is dressed in royal robes, to beat a large drum, and make the following proclamation:—'The Bodhisattva, during three Asaṅkhyeya-kalpas[1], manifested his activity, and did not spare his own life. He gave up kingdom, city, wife, and son; he plucked out his eyes and gave them to another[2]; he cut off a piece of his flesh to ransom the life of a dove[2]; he cut off his head and gave it as an alms[3]; he gave his body to feed a starving tigress[3]; he grudged not his marrow and brains. In many such ways as these did he undergo pain for the sake of all living. And so it was, that, having become Buddha, he continued in the world for forty-five years, preaching his Law, teaching and transforming, so that those who had no rest found rest, and the unconverted were converted. When his connexion with the living was completed[4], he attained to pari-nirvâṇa (and died). Since that event, for 1497 years, the light of the world has gone out[5], and all living beings have had long-continued sadness. Behold! ten days after this, Buddha's tooth will be brought forth, and taken to the Abhayagiri-vihâra. Let all and each, whether

---

[1] A Kalpa, we have seen, denotes a great period of time; a period during which a physical universe is formed and destroyed. Asaṅkhyeya denotes the highest sum for which a conventional term exists;—according to Chinese calculations equal to one followed by seventeen ciphers; according to Thibetan and Singhalese, equal to one followed by ninety-seven ciphers. Every Mahâ-kalpa consists of four Asaṅkhyeya-kalpas. Eitel, p. 15.

[2] See chapter ix.

[3] See chapter xi.

[4] He had been born in the Śâkya house, to do for the world what the character of all his past births required, and he had done it.

[5] They could no more see him, the World-honoured one. Compare the Sacred Books of the East, vol. xi, Buddhist Suttas, pp. 89, 121, and note on p. 89.

monks or laics, who wish to amass merit for themselves, make the roads smooth and in good condition, grandly adorn the lanes and by-ways, and provide abundant store of flowers and incense to be used as offerings to it.'

When this proclamation is over, the king exhibits, so as to line both sides of the road, the five hundred different bodily forms in which the Bodhisattva has in the course of his history appeared:—here as Sudâna[1], there as Sâma[2]; now as the king of elephants[3], and then as a stag or a horse[3]. All these figures are brightly coloured and grandly executed, looking as if they were alive. After this the tooth of Buddha is brought forth, and is carried along in the middle of the road. Everywhere on the way offerings are presented to it, and thus it arrives at the hall of Buddha in the Abhayagiri-vihâra. There monks and laics are

---

[1] Sudâna or Sudatta was the name of the Bodhisattva in the birth which preceded his appearance as Śâkyamuni or Gotama, when he became the Supreme Buddha. This period is known as the Vessantara Jâtaka, of which Hardy, M. B., pp. 116–124, gives a long account; see also 'Buddhist Birth Stories,' the Nidâna Kathâ, p. 158. In it, as Sudâna, he fulfilled 'the Perfections,' his distinguishing attribute being entire self-renunciation and alms-giving, so that in the Nidâna Kathâ he is made to say ('Buddhist Birth Stories,' p. 158):—

'This earth, unconscious though she be, and ignorant of joy or grief,
Even she by my free-giving's mighty power was shaken seven times.'

Then, when he passed away, he appeared in the Tushita heaven, to enter in due time the womb of Mahâ-mâyâ, and be born as Śâkyamuni.

[2] I take the name Sâma from Beal's revised version. He says in a note that the Sâma Jâtaka, as well as the Vessantara, is represented in the Sâñchi sculptures. But what the Sâma Jâtaka was I do not yet know. But adopting this name, the two Chinese characters in the text should be translated 'the change into Sâma.' Rémusat gives for them, 'la transformation en éclair;' Beal, in his first version, 'his appearance as a bright flash of light;' Giles, 'as a flash of lightning;' my own first version was 'as the changing flashes of lightning.' Julien's Méthode does not give the phonetic value in Sanskrit of 睒.

[3] In an analysis of the number of times and the different forms in which Śâkyamuni had appeared in his Jâtaka births, given by Hardy (M. B., p. 100), it is said that he had appeared six times as an elephant; ten times as a deer; and four times as a horse.

collected in crowds. They burn incense, light lamps, and perform all the prescribed services, day and night without ceasing, till ninety days have been completed, when (the tooth) is returned to the vihâra within the city. On fast-days the door of that vihâra is opened, and the forms of ceremonial reverence are observed according to the rules.

Forty le to the east of the Abhayagiri-vihâra there is a hill, with a vihâra on it, called the Chaitya[1], where there may be 2000 monks. Among them there is a Śramaṇa of great virtue, named Dharma-gupta[2], honoured and looked up to by all the kingdom. He has lived for more than forty years in an apartment of stone, constantly showing such gentleness of heart, that he has brought snakes and rats to stop together in the same room, without doing one another any harm.

CHAPTER XXXIX.

CREMATION OF AN ARHAT. SERMON OF A DEVOTEE.

SOUTH of the city seven le there is a vihâra, called the Mahâ-vihâra, where 3000 monks reside. There had been among them a Śramaṇa, of such lofty virtue, and so holy and pure in his observance of the disciplinary rules, that the people all surmised that he was an Arhat. When he drew near his end, the king came to examine into the point; and having assembled the monks according to rule, asked whether the bhikshu had attained to the full degree of Wisdom[3]. They answered in the affirmative, saying that he was an Arhat. The king accordingly, when he died, buried him after the fâshion of an Arhat, as the regular rules prescribed.

---

[1] Chaitya is a general term designating all places and objects of religious worship which have a reference to ancient Buddhas, and including therefore Stûpas and temples as well as sacred relics, pictures, statues, &c. It is defined as 'a fane,' 'a place for worship and presenting offerings.' Eitel, p. 141. The hill referred to is the sacred hill of Mihintale, about eight miles due east of the Bo tree;—Davids' Buddhism, pp. 230, 231.

[2] Eitel says (p. 31): 'A famous ascetic, the founder of a school, which flourished in Ceylon, A.D. 400.' But Fâ-hien gives no intimation of Dharmagupta's founding a school.

[3] Possibly, 'and asked the bhikshu,' &c. I prefer the other way of construing, however.

Four or five le east from the vihâra there was reared a great pile of fire-wood, which might be more than thirty cubits square, and the same in height. Near the top were laid sandal, aloe, and other kinds of fragrant wood.

On the four sides (of the pile) they made steps by which to ascend it. With clean white hair-cloth, almost like silk, they wrapped (the body) round and round[1]. They made a large carriage-frame, in form like our funeral car, but without the dragons and fishes[2].

At the time of the cremation, the king and the people, in multitudes from all quarters, collected together, and presented offerings of flowers and incense. While they were following the car to the burial-ground[3], the king himself presented flowers and incense. When this was finished, the car was lifted on the pile, all over which oil of sweet basil was poured, and then a light was applied. While the fire was blazing, every one, with a reverent heart, pulled off his upper garment, and threw it, with his feather-fan and umbrella, from a distance into the midst of the flames, to assist the burning. When the cremation was over, they collected and preserved the bones, and proceeded to erect a tope. Fâ-hien had not arrived in time (to see the distinguished Shaman) alive, and only saw his burial.

At that time the king[4], who was a sincere believer in the Law of Buddha and wished to build a new vihâra for the monks, first convoked a great

---

[1] It seems strange that this should have been understood as a wrapping of the immense pyre with the cloth. There is nothing in the text to necessitate such a version, but the contrary. Compare 'Buddhist Suttas,' pp. 92, 93.

[2] See the description of a funeral car and its decorations in the Sacred Books of the East, vol. xxviii, the Lî *K*î, Book XIX. Fâ-hien's 此間, 'in this (country),' which I have expressed by 'our,' shows that whatever notes of this cremation he had taken at the time, the account in the text was composed after his return to China, and when he had the usages there in his mind and perhaps before his eyes. This disposes of all difficulty occasioned by the 'dragons' and 'fishes.' The 耳 at the end is merely the concluding particle.

[3] The pyre served the purpose of a burial-ground or grave, and hence our author writes of it as such.

[4] This king must have been Mahâ-nâna (A. D. 410–432). In the time of his

assembly. After giving the monks a meal of rice, and presenting his offerings (on the occasion), he selected a pair of first-rate oxen, the horns of which were grandly decorated with gold, silver, and the precious substances. A golden plough had been provided, and the king himself turned up a furrow on the four sides of the ground within which the building was to be. He then endowed the community of the monks with the population, fields, and houses, writing the grant on plates of metal, (to the effect) that from that time onwards, from generation to generation, no one should venture to annul or alter it.

In this country Fâ-hien heard an Indian devotee, who was reciting a Sûtra from the pulpit, say:—'Buddha's alms-bowl was at first in Vaiśâlî, and now it is in Gandhâra[1]. After so many hundred years' (he gave, when Fâ-hien heard him, the exact number of years, but he has forgotten it), 'it will go to Western Tukhâra[2]; after so many hundred years, to Khoten; after so many hundred years, to Kharachar[3]; after so many hundred years, to the land of Han; after so many hundred years, it will come to Siṇhala; and after so many hundred years, it will return to Central India. After that, it will ascend to the Tushita heaven; and when the Bodhisattva Maitreya sees it, he will say with a sigh, "The alms-bowl of Śâkyamuni Buddha is come;" and with all the devas he will present to it flowers and incense for seven days. When these have expired, it will return to Jambudvîpa, where it will be received by the king of the sea nâgas, and taken into his nâga palace. When Maitreya shall be about to attain to perfect Wisdom (and become Buddha), it will again separate into four bowls[4], which will return to the top of mount Anna[4], whence they came. After Maitreya has become

---

predecessor, Upatissa (A.D. 368–410), the piṭakas were first translated into Singhalese. Under Mahâ-nâna, Buddhaghosha wrote his commentaries. Both were great builders of vihâras. See the Mahâvaṇśa, pp. 247, foll.

[1] See chapter xii. Fâ-hien had seen it at Purushapura, which Eitel says was 'the ancient capital of Gandhâra.'

[2] Western Tukhâra (西 肢) is the same probably as the Tukhâra (肢支) of chapter xii, a king of which is there described as trying to carry off the bowl from Purushapura.

[3] North of the Bosteng lake at the foot of the Thien-shan range (E. H., p. 56).

[4] See note 3, p. 35. Instead of 'Anna' the Chinese recensions have Vîna;

Buddha, the four deva kings will again think of the Buddha (with their bowls as they did in the case of the previous Buddha). The thousand Buddhas of this Bhadra-kalpa, indeed, will all use the same alms-bowl; and when the bowl has disappeared, the Law of Buddha will go on gradually to be extinguished. After that extinction has taken place, the life of man will be shortened, till it is only a period of five years. During this period of a five years' life, rice, butter, and oil will all vanish away, and men will become exceedingly wicked. The grass and trees which they lay hold of will change into swords and clubs, with which they will hurt, cut, and kill one another. Those among them on whom there is blessing will withdraw from society among the hills; and when the wicked have exterminated one another, they will again come forth, and say among themselves, "The men of former times enjoyed a very great longevity; but through becoming exceedingly wicked, and doing all lawless things, the length of our life has been shortened and reduced even to five years. Let us now unite together in the practice of what is good, cherishing a gentle and sympathising heart, and carefully cultivating good faith and righteousness. When each one in this way practises that faith and righteousness, life will go on to double its length till it reaches 80,000 years. When Maitreya appears in the world, and begins to turn the wheel of his Law, he will in the first place save those among the disciples of the Law left by the Śâkya who have quitted their families, and those who have accepted the three Refuges, undertaken the five Prohibitions and the eight Abstinences, and given offerings to the three Precious Ones; secondly and thirdly, he will save those between whom and conversion there is a connexion transmitted from the past[1].''

(Such was the discourse), and Fâ-hien wished to write it down as a portion of doctrine; but the man said, 'This is taken from no Sûtra, it is only the utterance of my own mind.'

---

but Vîna or Vînataka, and Ana for Sudarśana are names of one or other of the concentric circles of rocks surrounding mount Meru, the fabled home of the deva guardians of the bowl.

[1] That is, those whose Karma in the past should be rewarded by such conversion in the present.

CHAPTER XL.

AFTER TWO YEARS TAKES SHIP FOR CHINA. DISASTROUS PASSAGE TO JAVA; AND THENCE TO CHINA; ARRIVES AT SHAN-TUNG; AND GOES TO NANKING. CONCLUSION OR L'ENVOI BY ANOTHER WRITER.

FÂ-HIEN abode in this country two years; and, in addition (to his acquisitions in Patna), succeeded in getting a copy of the Vinaya-piṭaka of the Mahîśâsakâḥ (school)[1]; the Dîrghâgama and Saṃyuktâgama[2] (Sûtras); and also the Saṃyukta-sañchaya-piṭaka[3];—all being works unknown in the land of Han. Having obtained these Sanskrit works, he took passage in a large merchantman, on board of which there were more than 200 men, and to which was attached by a rope a smaller vessel, as a provision against damage or injury to the large one from the perils of the navigation. With a favourable wind, they proceeded eastwards for three days, and then they encountered a great wind. The vessel sprang a leak and the water came in. The merchants wished to go to the smaller vessel; but the men on board it, fearing that too many would come, cut the connecting rope. The merchants were greatly alarmed, feeling their risk of instant death. Afraid that the vessel would fill, they took their bulky goods and threw

---

[1] No. 1122 in Nanjio's Catalogue, translated into Chinese by Buddhajîva and a Chinese Śramaṇa about A.D. 425. Mahîśâsakâḥ means 'the school of the transformed earth,' or 'the sphere within which the Law of Buddha is influential.' The school is one of the subdivisions of the Sarvâstivâdâḥ.

[2] Nanjio's 545 and 504. The Âgamas are Sûtras of the hînayâna, divided, according to Eitel, pp. 4, 5, into four classes, the first or Dîrghâgamas (long Âgamas) being treatises on right conduct, while the third class contains the Saṃyuktâgamas (mixed Âgamas).

[3] Meaning 'Miscellaneous Collections;' a sort of fourth Piṭaka. See Nanjio's fourth division of the Canon, containing Indian and Chinese miscellaneous works. But Dr. Davids says that no work of this name is known either in Sanskrit or Pâli literature.

them into the water. Fâ-hien also took his pitcher[1] and washing-basin, with some other articles, and cast them into the sea; but fearing that the merchants would cast overboard his books and images, he could only think with all his heart of Kwan-she-yin[2], and commit his life to (the protection of) the church of the land of Han[3], (saying in effect), 'I have travelled far in search of our Law. Let me, by your dread and supernatural (power), return from my wanderings, and reach my resting-place!'

In this way the tempest[4] continued day and night, till on the thirteenth day the ship was carried to the side of an island, where, on the ebbing of the tide, the place of the leak was discovered, and it was stopped, on which the voyage was resumed. On the sea (hereabouts) there are many pirates, to meet with whom is speedy death. The great ocean spreads out, a boundless expanse. There is no knowing east or west; only by observing the sun, moon, and stars was it possible to go forward. If the weather were dark and rainy, (the ship) went as she was carried by the wind, without any definite course. In the darkness of the night, only the great waves were to be seen, breaking on one another, and emitting a brightness like that of fire, with huge turtles and other monsters of the deep (all about). The merchants were full of terror, not knowing where they were going. The sea was deep and bottomless, and there was no place where they could drop anchor and stop. But when the sky became clear, they could tell east and west, and (the ship) again went forward in

---

[1] We have in the text a phonetisation of the Sanskrit Kuṇḍikâ, which is explained in Eitel by the two characters that follow, as='washing basin,' but two things evidently are intended.

[2] See note 5, p. 46.

[3] At his novitiate Fâ-hien had sought the refuge of the 'three Precious Ones' (the three Refuges [三 歸] of last chapter), of which the congregation or body of the monks was one; and here his thoughts turn naturally to the branch of it in China. His words in his heart were not exactly words of prayer, but very nearly so.

[4] In the text 大 風, tâ-fung, 'the great wind,'=the typhoon.

the right direction. If she had come on any hidden rock, there would have been no way of escape.

After proceeding in this way for rather more than ninety days, they arrived at a country called Java-dvîpa, where various forms of error and Brahmanism are flourishing, while Buddhism in it is not worth speaking of. After staying there for five months, (Fâ-hien) again embarked in another large merchantman, which also had on board more than 200 men. They carried provisions for fifty days, and commenced the voyage on the sixteenth day of the fourth month.

Fâ-hien kept his retreat on board the ship. They took a course to the north-east, intending to fetch Kwang-chow. After more than a month, when the night-drum had sounded the second watch, they encountered a black wind and tempestuous rain, which threw the merchants and passengers into consternation. Fâ-hien again with all his heart directed his thoughts to Kwan-she-yin and the monkish communities of the land of Han; and, through their dread and mysterious protection, was preserved to day-break. After day-break, the Brahmans deliberated together and said, 'It is having this Śramaṇa on board which has occasioned our misfortune and brought us this great and bitter suffering. Let us land the bhikshu and place him on some island-shore. We must not for the sake of one man allow ourselves to be exposed to such imminent peril.' A patron of Fâ-hien, however, said to them, 'If you land the bhikshu, you must at the same time land me; and if you do not, then you must kill me. If you land this Śramaṇa, when I get to the land of Han, I will go to the king, and inform against you. The king also reveres and believes the Law of Buddha, and honours the bhikshus.' The merchants hereupon were perplexed, and did not dare immediately to land (Fâ-hien).

At this time the sky continued very dark and gloomy, and the sailing-masters looked at one another and made mistakes. More than seventy days passed (from their leaving Java), and the provisions and water were nearly exhausted. They used the salt-water of the sea for cooking, and carefully divided the (fresh) water, each man getting two pints. Soon the whole was nearly gone, and the merchants took counsel and said, 'At the ordinary rate of sailing we ought to have reached Kwang-chow, and now the time is passed by many days;—

must we not have held a wrong course?' Immediately they directed the ship to the north-west, looking out for land; and after sailing day and night for twelve days, they reached the shore on the south of mount Lâo[1], on the borders of the prefecture of Ch'ang-kwang[1], and immediately got good water and vegetables. They had passed through many perils and hardships, and had been in a state of anxious apprehension for many days together; and now suddenly arriving at this shore, and seeing those (well-known) vegetables, the lei and kwoh[2], they knew indeed that it was the land of Han. Not seeing, however, any inhabitants nor any traces of them, they did not know whereabouts they were. Some said that they had not yet got to Kwang-chow, and others that they had passed it. Unable to come to a definite conclusion, (some of them) got into a small boat and entered a creek, to look for some one of whom they might ask what the place was. They found two hunters, whom they brought back with them, and then called on Fâ-hien to act as interpreter and question them. Fâ-hien first spoke assuringly to them, and then slowly and distinctly asked them, 'Who are you?' They replied, 'We are disciples of Buddha?' He then asked, 'What are you looking for among these hills?' They began to lie[3], and said,

---

[1] They had got to the south of the Shan-tung promontory, and the foot of mount Lâo, which still rises under the same name on the extreme south of the peninsula, east from Keâo Chow, and having the district of Tseih-mih on the east of it. All the country there is included in the present Phing-too Chow of the department Lâe-chow. The name Phing-too dates from the Han dynasty, but under the dynasty of the After Ch'e (後 齊), (A.D. 479-501), it was changed into Ch'ang-kwang. Fâ-hien may have lived, and composed the narrative of his travels, after the change of name was adopted. See the Topographical Tables of the different Dynasties (歷代沿革表), published in 1815.

[2] What these vegetables exactly were it is difficult to say; and there are different readings of the characters for them. Williams' Dictionary, under kwoh, brings the two names together in a phrase, but the rendering of it is simply 'a soup of simples.' For two or three columns here, however, the text appears to me confused and imperfect.

[3] I suppose these men were really hunters; and, when brought before Fâ-hien, because he was a Śramaṇa, they thought they would please him by saying

'To-morrow is the fifteenth day of the seventh month. We wanted to get some peaches to present[1] to Buddha.' He asked further, 'What country is this?' They replied, 'This is the border of the prefecture of Ch'ang-kwang, a part of Ts'ing-chow under the (ruling) House of Tsin.' When they heard this, the merchants were glad, immediately asked for (a portion of) their money and goods, and sent men to Ch'ang-kwang city.

The prefect Le E was a reverent believer in the Law of Buddha. When he heard that a Śramaṇa had arrived in a ship across the sea, bringing with him books and images, he immediately came to the sea-shore with an escort to meet (the traveller), and receive the books and images, and took them back with him to the seat of his government. On this the merchants went back in the direction of Yang-chow[2]; (but) when (Fâ-hien) arrived at Ts'ing-chow, (the prefect there)[3] begged him (to remain with him) for a winter and a summer. After the summer retreat was ended, Fâ-hien, having been separated for a long time from his (fellow-)masters, wished to hurry to Ch'ang-gan; but as the business which he had in hand was important, he went south to the Capital[4]; and at an interview with the masters (there) exhibited the Sûtras and the collection of the Vinaya (which he had procured).

After Fâ-hien set out from Ch'ang-gan, it took him six years to reach

---

they were disciples of Buddha. But what had disciples of Buddha to do with hunting and taking life? They were caught in their own trap, and said they were looking for peaches.

[1] The Chinese character here has occurred twice before, but in a different meaning and connexion. Rémusat, Beal, and Giles take it as equivalent to 'to sacrifice.' But his followers do not 'sacrifice' to Buddha. That is a priestly term, and should not be employed of anything done at Buddhistic services.

[2] Probably the present department of Yang-chow in Keang-soo; but as I have said in a previous note, the narrative does not go on so clearly as it generally does.

[3] Was, or could, this prefect be Le E?

[4] Probably not Ch'ang-gan, but Nan-king, which was the capital of the Eastern Tsin dynasty under another name.

Central India[1]; stoppages there extended over (other) six years; and on his return it took him three years to reach Ts'ing-chow. The countries through which he passed were a few under thirty. From the sandy desert westwards on to India, the beauty of the dignified demeanour of the monkhood and of the transforming influence of the Law was beyond the power of language fully to describe; and reflecting how our masters had not heard any complete account of them, he therefore (went on) without regarding his own poor life, or (the dangers to be encountered) on the sea upon his return, thus incurring hardships and difficulties in a double form. He was fortunate enough, through the dread power of the three Honoured Ones[1], to receive help and protection in his perils; and therefore he wrote out an account of his experiences, that worthy readers might share with him in what he had heard and said[1].

It was in the year Keah-yin[2], the twelfth year of the period E-he of the

---

[1] The whole of this paragraph is probably Fâ-hien's own conclusion of his narrative. The second half of the second sentence, both in sentiment and style in the Chinese text, seems to necessitate our ascribing it to him, writing on the impulse of his own thoughts, in the same indirect form which he adopted for his whole narrative. There are, however, two peculiar phraseologies in it which might suggest the work of another hand. For the name India, where the first [1] is placed, a character is employed which is similarly applied nowhere else; and again, 'the three Honoured Ones,' at which the second [1] is placed, must be the same as 'the three Precious Ones,' which we have met with so often; unless we suppose that 三尊 is printed in all the revisions for 世尊, 'the World-honoured one,' which has often occurred. On the whole, while I accept this paragraph as Fâ-hien's own, I do it with some hesitation. That the following and concluding paragraph is from another hand, there can be no doubt. And it is as different as possible in style from the simple and straightforward narrative of Fâ-hien.

[2] There is an error of date here, for which it is difficult to account. The year Keah-yin was A.D. 414; but that was the tenth year of the period E-he, and not the twelfth, the cyclical designation of which was Ping-shin. According to the preceding paragraph, Fâ-hien's travels had occupied him fifteen years, so that counting from A.D. 399, the year Ke-hâe, as that in which he set out, the year of his getting to Ts'ing-chow would have been Kwei-chow, the ninth year of the

(Eastern) Tsin dynasty, the year-star being in Virgo-Libra, in the summer, at the close of the period of retreat, that I met the devotee Fâ-hien. On his arrival I lodged him with myself in the winter study[1], and there, in our meetings for conversation, I asked him again and again about his travels. The man was modest and complaisant, and answered readily according to the truth. I thereupon advised him to enter into details where he had at first only given a summary, and he proceeded to relate all things in order from the beginning to the end. He said himself, 'When I look back on what I have gone through, my heart is involuntarily moved, and the perspiration flows forth. That I encountered danger and trod the most perilous places, without thinking of or sparing myself, was because I had a definite aim, and thought of nothing but to do my best in my simplicity and straightforwardness. Thus it was that I exposed my life where death seemed inevitable, if I might accomplish but a ten-thousandth part of what I hoped.' These words affected me in turn, and I thought:—'This man is one of those who have seldom been seen from ancient times to the present. Since the Great Doctrine flowed on to the East there has been no one to be compared with Hien in his forgetfulness of self and search for the Law. Henceforth I know that the influence of sincerity finds no obstacle, how-

---

period E-he; and we might join on 'This year Keah-yin' to that paragraph, as the date at which the narrative was written out for the bamboo-tablets and the silk, and then begins the Envoy, 'In the twelfth year of E-he.' This would remove the error as it stands at present, but unfortunately there is a particle at the end of the second date (矣), which seems to tie the twelfth year of E-he to Keah-yin, as another designation of it. The 'year-star' is the planet Jupiter, the revolution of which, in twelve years, constitutes 'a great year.' Whether it would be possible to fix exactly by mathematical calculation in what year Jupiter was in the Chinese zodiacal sign embracing part of both Virgo and Scorpio, and thereby help to solve the difficulty of the passage, I do not know, and in the meantime must leave that difficulty as I have found it.

[1] We do not know who the writer of the Envoy was. 'The winter study or library' would be the name of the apartment in his monastery or house, where he sat and talked with Fâ-hien.

ever great, which it does not overcome, and that force of will does not fail to accomplish whatever service it undertakes. Does not the accomplishing of such service arise from forgetting (and disregarding) what is (generally) considered as important, and attaching importance to what is (generally) forgotten?'

INDEX.

Â-e (Asita, ṛishi), page 65.
Â-le, 54.
Abhayagiri monastery, 102, 105, 106, 107. Hall of Buddha in, and statue of jade, 102, 103.
Abhidharma, 10 et al.
Ajâtaśatru (king), 76, 81, 82, 85.
Alms-bowl of Buddha, 34, 35, 109, 110.
Âmbapâlî, 72.
Anâgâmin, 57, 86.
Ânanda, 33, 44, 45, 72, 74, 83; death of, in Samâdhi, 75–77.
Âṅgulimâlya, 56.
Anna (mount), 109.
Anuruddha, 48.
Arhan, the, or Arhat (in Chinese Lo-han), 24, 40, 57, 71, 75, 86. Cremation of an Arhat, 107, 108.
Ârya, 57.
Asaṅkhyeya-kalpa, 105.
Aśoka, 31, 50; his spirit-built palace, and halls, 77; his brother, 77; his great tope and inscription, 80; his vihâra and pillar, 50, 51; his city and pillar of Ne-le, 80; wished to build 84,000 topes, 69; legend of his naraka, 90–92.

Bhikshu, 13, 29, 75, 83, 86, 91, 92, 113. Suicide of, 86. Bhikshuṇî, 45.
Bimbisâra (king), 81, 82.
Bo tree, the, in Ceylon, 103, 104. In Gayâ, 88. Both are called in mistake by Fâ-hien the patra tree.
Bodhisattva, 19. Legends of Buddha, when Bodhisattva, 30, 31, 32, 38, 73, 74, 105. Maitreya Bodhisattva, 25.
Books of Discipline, the. See Vinaya.
Brahma (king), the first person of the Brahmanical Trimurti, 49, 89.
Brahmans, 47, 55, 60, 61. The Brahman Râdha-sâmi, 78.
Buddha, incarnation of the, 65; incidents of his early life, 65, 66; where he renounced the world, 70; where he died, 70; where he endured austerities, 87; legends of that time, 87, 88. His attainment of the Buddhaship, 89; first labours afterwards, 89. In Ceylon, 101; his wonderful stride and footprint, 102. Buddha's preaching, 54, 66.
Buddhism, Fâ-hien's name for, 30.
Buddhists, different estimates of the number of, 5–8.

Central India, or the Middle Kingdom, 28. Condition and customs of, 42, 43.
Chakravartti king, 49, 90.
Champâ, 100. Topes and monasteries in, 100.
Chañchamana, 60.
Chaṇḍaka, 70.
Chaṇḍâlas, 43.
Ch'ang-gan, 9, 10, 115.
Chang K'een, 27.
Chang-yih, 11.

Charcoal tope, the, 70.
Che-yen (pilgrim), 11, 15.
China, or the land of Han, 13, 24, 58, 100, 109, 113.
Council in Śrataparṇa cavern, 85; of Vaiśâli, 75.

Dakshiṇa, 96–98.
Dâna and dânapati, 11, 52.
Danta-kâshṭha, legend of Buddha's, 54, 55.
Desert of Gobi, 12.
Deva, or Brahmanic god, 19, 50, 79.
Devadatta, 60, 86; followers of, 62.
Devâlaya, 'The Shadow Covered,' 60, 61.
Devaloka, 25.
Dharma, the Law, one of the constituents of Buddhism, 28 et al.
Dharma-gupta, 106, 107.
Dîpâṅkara Buddha, 38.
Discourse or sermon of a devotee in Ceylon, 110.
Dragons or nâgas, 29, 67, 101; the dragon of the Râma tope, 69; the white-eared dragon, 52; Elâpattra, 96.

E-he (period), 116.
Endowments of the monkish communities, and offerings to them, 22, 23, 43, 44, 108, 109.

Fâ-hien. His surname, and notices of his early life, 1, 2; lived to the age of eighty-eight, 2, 3. Genuineness of his narrative, 3, 4. Different recensions of it, and especially the Corean text appended to this volume, 4. Stages of his travels:—Ch'ang-gan, 10; Lung, 10; kingdom of K'een-kwei, 10; that of Now-t'an, 10; Chang-yih, 11; T'un-hwang, 11; desert of Gobi, 12; Shen-shen, 12; Woo-e, 14; Yu-teen, 16; Tsze-hoh, 21; Yu-hwuy, 21; K'eeh-ch'â, 22; T'o-leih, 24; crosses the Indus, 26; Woo-chang, or Udyâna, 28; Soo-ho-to, or Swastene, 29; Gandhâra, 31; Takshaśilâ, 32; Purushapura, or Peshâwur, 33; He-lo, or Hidda, in Nagâra, 36; Nagâra, 38–40; Little Snowy mountains, 40; Lo-e, 41; Poh-nâ, 41; recrosses the Indus, 41; Pe-t'oo, or Bhida, 41; Mathurâ, or Muttra, 42; Saṅkâśya, 47; Kanyâkubja, or Canouge, 53; Â-le, 54; Shâ-che, 54; Śrâvastî in Kośala, 55; Too-wei, 63; Na-pei-keâ, 64; Kapilavastu, 64; Râma, 68; Kuśanagara, 70; Vaiśâlî, 72; confluence of the five rivers, 75; Pâṭaliputtra, or Patna, 77; Râjagṛiha, 80; Nâla, 81; New Râjagṛiha, 81; Gṛidhra-kûṭa hill, 83; Śrataparṇa cave, 85; Gayâ, 87; mount Gurupada, 92; Vârâṇasî, or Benâres, 93; Kâśî, 94; Kauśâmbî, 96; Patna, 98; Champâ, 100; Tâmaliptî, 100; Singhala, or Ceylon, 101; Java, 113; Shantung, in China, 114; the Capital, 115.
First image made of Buddha, 57.
Foo Kung-sun, 15.
Four great topes in North India, 32; in Central India, 90.
Four places of regular occurrence in the history of all Buddhas, 68.
Four spiritual truths, and four classes of disciples, 57.

Gandhâra, 31, 33, 109.
Ganges, 54, 93, 100.
Gayâ, 87–90.

Gomati monastery, 17.
Gośîrsha Chandana wood, 39, 57.
Gṛidhra-kûṭa hill, 80, 82. Legends connected with, 83. Fâ-hien spends a night on, 83.
Grove of the Getting of Eyes, 58, 59.
Gurupada (mount), 92.

Habits of the Khoteners, 16, 17.
Hall of Buddha, 20, 102.
Han, the land of. See China.
He-lo, 36.
Hînayâna, 14, 15, 23, 41, et al.
Ho-shang, name of, 58.
Hwăng-che (period), 9.
Hwuy-keen (pilgrim), 11, 15.
Hwuy-king (pilgrim), 9, 18, 22, 29, 36. Death of, 40, 41.
Hwuy-tah (pilgrim), 18, 29, 36.
Hwuy-wei (pilgrim), 10, 15.
Hwuy-ying (pilgrim), 10. Death of, 36.

India, 10, 14. (North), 24, 28, 29. (Central), 28, 42. (South), 47.
Indus, the, 26. Crossing it, 26; re-crossing it, 41.

Jambudvîpa, 34, 48, 80.
Jâtaka stories, 30, 31, 32, 73, 74, et al.
Jetavana vihâra, 56; burning of the, 57. Sympathy of the monks at, with the pilgrims, 58. Park of the, 59.
Jîvaka, 82.

Kanishka (king), 33; and his tope, 34.
Kanyâkubja, or Canouge, 53, 54.
Kan Ying, 27.
Kâo-ch'ang, 15.
Kapilavastu, 64–68.
Karaṇḍa Bamboo garden (Karaṇḍa Veṇuvana), 84.
Kâśî, 94.
Kaśyapa brothers and their disciples, 89.
Kaśyapa Buddha's entire skeleton, 93.
Kauṇḍinya and his companions, 94, 95.
Kauśâmbî, 96.
Keah-yin (year), 116.
K'eeh-ch'â, 18, 22.
K'een-kwei, 10.
Ke-hâe (year), 9.
Kharachar, 109.
Khoten, 16–20, 109.
King Prasenajit, 55.
King's New monastery, 19.
Kophene, 21.
Kośala, 55.
Kwang-chow, 114.
Kwan-she-yin, 46, 112, 113.

Le E (prefect), 115.
Le Hâo, 12.
Legends of Buddha in North India, 29, 30, 39; as Bodhisattva, 31. Of his danta-kâshṭha, 54, 55.
Legends of Takshaśilâ, 32.
Legends of topes and monastery, 53, 73.
Lichchhavis, 71, 72, 76.
Little Snowy mountains, 40.
Lo-e, 41.
Lumbinî (garden), 67. Birth of Buddha in, 67.
Lung, 10.

Madhyamayâna, 14.
Mahâkaśyapa, 45, 85.
Mahâ-maudgalyâyana (Mugalan), 44, 48, 82.
Mahâ-prajâpatî, 55, 66.
Mahâyâna, 14, 16, 21, 41, et al.
Maitreya Bodhisattva, 25; statue of, 25, 28, 109.

Mañjuśrî, 46, 79 (a Brahman).
Mâra, king, 74; Piśuna, 83; 88.
Mathurâ, or Muttra, 42.
Merchants (five hundred), 89.
Monasteries, or Saṅghârâmas, 17, 28, et al.
Monastery (Gomati), 17.
Monastery of the Great Heap, 52.
Monastery (Pigeon), 96–98.
Monkish customs, 44–47.
Monkish food out of the ordinary hours, 44.
Monks (4000 in Shen-shen), 13; (4000 in Woo-e), 15; (several myriads in Khoten), 15. Influence of the, 42. Quinquennial assembly of, 22, 23.
Mother of Buddha (Mahâ-mâyâ), 48, 56, 65.
Muchilinda (dragon), 89.

Nâgara, 29, 36.
Nâla, 81.
Nanda, 65.
Naraka, 90.
Ne-le city and pillar, 80.
New Râjagṛiha, 81.
Ninety-six sorts of erroneous views, 62.
Nirgrantha, the, 82.
Nirvâṇa, 14, 27, 33, et al.
Now-t'an, 10.

Onion mountains, 20, 21, 23, 24.

Pâo-yun (pilgrim), 11, 15, 36.
Pâramitâs, the, 46; Prajñâ-pâramitâ, 46.
Pari-nirvâṇa, 33, 57, 73.
Park of 'The ṛishi's Deer-wild,' 94.
Pâṭaliputtra, or Patna, 77; monasteries of, 78, 79; hospitals and dispensaries of, 79, 97–99. Manuscripts copied there, 98–99; the Mahâsâṅghika rules, Sarvâstivâdâḥ rules, Saṃyuktâbhidharma-hṛidaya-(śâstra), Sûtra of 2500 gâthas, the Parinirvâṇa-vaipulya Sûtra, Mahâsâṅghikâḥ Abhidharma, 99.
Pe-t'oo, or Bhida, 41.
P'ing (king of Chow dynasty), 27.
Plain (Central and South India), 47.
Poh-nâ, 41.
Poonah, or Jumna river, 42.
Prasenajit. See King
Pratyeka Buddhas, 40, 53, 74.
Procession of images at Khoten, 16–19; at Patna, 79; in Ceylon, 106, 107.
Purushapura, or Peshâwur, 33.

Quinquennial assembly of monks, 22.

Râhula, 46.
Râjagṛiha (new and old) legends and incidents, 80–86.
Râma and its tope, 68, 69.
Relics of Buddha:—spittoon, 23; alms-bowl, 23, 34, 35, 89, 109; tooth, 23, 105, 107; skull-bone, 36, 37; pewter staff, 39; Saṅghâli, or Saṅghâṭi, 39; hair and nails, 39 et al.; shadow, 39, 88.
Retreat (the summer), 10, 11, 22, 29, 113, 117, et al.

Śakra, 30, 34, 49, 50, 60, 80, 81.
Sâma, 106.
Samâdhi, 76.
Saṅghâli. See Relics.
Săng-king (pilgrim), 11, 36.
Săng-shâo (pilgrim), 11, 21.
Saṅkâśya, 47.
Śâriputtra, 44, 81, 82.
Shâ-che, 54.
Shadow of Buddha. See Relics.
Shay-e, 63.
Shen-shen, 12.
Shikshâpada, or ten commandments, 46.

Singhala, or Ceylon, 100–111. Manuscripts obtained in, 111.
Śmaśânam, 84.
Snow mountains, 24.
Soo-ho-to (Swastene), 29, 30.
Śramaṇa (Śraman, Shâ-măn), 14 et al.
Śrâmaṇera, 45, 69, 70.
Śrataparṇa cave, or cave of the First Council, 84, 85.
Śrâvastî, 55, 56. Topes and legends of, 56–61.
Śrotâpannas, 67, 86.
Subhadra, 71.
Sudâna, 106.
Sudatta, 56.
Śuddhodana, 64.
Sympathy of Indian monks with pilgrims, 41.

Takshaśilâ, 32.
Tamâliptî, 100.
Tâo-ching (pilgrim), 9, 18, 29, 36, 99.
Tathâgata, 63.
Three Buddhas anterior to Śâkyamuni, 63, 64.
T'o-leih, or Darada, 24.
Topes, 17, 40, 53, et al. Buddha himself assisted in building a model tope, 39, 40.
Trayastriṃśas heaven, legend of Buddha's ascent to and descent from, 48, 49.
Treasuries of the monasteries in Ceylon, 103; rule regarding, 104.
Tripiṭaka, 10.
Trîsharaṇa, 46.
Ts'in, 15, 23.
Ts'ing-chow, 115.
Tsze-hoh, 21.
T'un-hwang, 11, 12.
Tushita heaven, 25.

Upâli, 66.
Upasena, 82.
Utpala bhikshuṇî, 49.

Vaiśakha (mother), 59.
Vaiśâlî, 72.
Vaiśyas, chiefs of, 38, 47.
Vanity of life and of the body, 54, 91.
Vârâṇasî, or Benâres, 94.
Vihâra, 36, 37, et al. King's grant of a new vihâra to monks in Ceylon, 108.
Vimoksha tope, 38.
Vinaya, or Books of Discipline, 9, 10, 98, et al.
Virûdhaha (Vaidûrya), king, 63, 67.

When the law of Buddha first went to the East, 27, 28.
Woo-chang, or Udyâna, 28, 29.
Woo-e, 14.

Yang-chow, 115.
Yang-low, 10.
Yu-hwuy, 21.
Yu-teen, or Khoten, 16.

留共冬齋，因講集之際，重問遊歷，其人恭順，言輒依實，由是先所略者勸令詳載，顯復具敍始末，自云，顧尋所經，不覺心動汗流，所以乘危履險，不惜此形者，蓋是志有所存，專其愚直，故投命於[1]必[2]死之地，以達萬一之冀。於是感歎，斯人以爲古今罕有，自大教東流，未有忘身求法如顯之比，然後知誠之所感，無窮否而不通，志之所將[3]，無功業而不成，成夫功業者，豈不由忘夫[4]所重，重夫所忘者哉。

法顯傳終

[1] After 於, S, M insert 不.　[2] S, M 全.　[3] S, M 奬.　[4] S, M 失.

言已過，莫知所定，卽乘小舶，入浦覓人，欲問其處，得兩獵人，卽將歸，令法顯譯語問之，法顯先安慰之，徐問汝是何人，答言，我是佛弟子，又問汝入山何所求，其便詭[1]言，明當七月十五日，欲取桃[2]臘佛，又問此是何國，答言，此青州長廣郡界，統屬晋[3]家，聞已，商人歡喜，卽乞其財物，遣人往長廣郡[4]太守李嶷，敬信佛法，聞有沙門，持經像，乘船泛海而至，卽將人從，來[5]至海邊，迎接經像，歸至郡治，商人，於是還向楊州，到[6]青州，請法顯一冬一夏。夏坐訖，法顯[7]離諸師，久欲趣長安，但所營事重，遂便南下向都，就師出經律藏[8]。法顯發長安，六年到中印[9]國，停經[10]六年，還經[11]三年，達青州，凡所遊履[12]，減三十國，沙河已西，迄于天竺，衆僧威儀法化之美，不可詳說，竊惟諸師，未[13]得備聞，是以不顧微命，浮海而還，艱難具更，幸蒙三尊威靈，危而得濟，故將[14]竹帛疏所經歷，欲令賢者同其聞見。〇是歲甲寅，晋義熙十二年矣，[15]歲在壽星，夏安居末，迎法顯道人，既至，

---

[1] J 說. [2] M 挑. W. [3] S 劉. [4] S, M omit. [5] S, M omit. [6] S 劉法; M 留法. [7] After 顯, S, M insert 遠. [8] S, M omit. [9] S, M omit. [10] S, M omit. [11] S, M omit. [12] S, M 歷. [13] J 來. [14] S, M omit. [15] S, M omit.

道婆羅門興盛，佛法不足言。停此國五月日，復隨他商人，大舶上，亦二百許人，賫五十日粮[1]，以四月十六日發，法顯於船上安居，東北行趣廣州，一月餘日，夜鼓二時，遇黑風暴雨，商人賈客，皆悉惶怖，法顯爾[2]時，亦一心念觀世音及漢地衆僧，蒙威神祐，得至天曉，曉已，諸婆羅門議言，坐載此沙門，使我不利，遭此大苦，當下比丘，置海島邊，不可爲一人令我等危嶮[3]，法顯[4]檀越言，汝若下此比丘，亦幷下我，不爾，便當殺我，如[5]其下此沙門，吾到漢地，當向國王言汝也，漢地王亦敬信佛法，重比丘僧，諸商人躊躇，不敢便下，于時天多連陰，海師相望僻誤，遂經七十餘日，粮食水漿欲盡，取海鹹水作食，分好水，人可得二升，遂便欲盡，商人議言，常行時，政[6]可五十日，便到廣州[7]，今已過期多日，將無僻耶，即便西北行求岸，晝夜十二日，到長廣郡界，牢山南岸，便得好水菜，但經涉險難，憂懼積日，忽得至此岸，見蔾[8]藋[8]菜，依然知是漢地，然不見人民及行跡，未知是何許，或言未至廣州，或

[1] S, M 糧. [2] Contracted form in text. [3] M 險. [4] After 顯, S, M insert 本. [5] S, M 汝. [6] S, M 正. [7] After 州, S, M insert 爾. [8] Should be 藜藿.

人云，此無經本，我心[1]口誦耳。○法顯住此國二年，更求得彌沙塞律藏本，得長阿含雜阿含，復得一部雜藏，此悉漢土所無者。得此梵本已，即載商人大船上，可有二百餘人，後係一小舶[2]海行艱嶮，以備大舶[2]毀壞，得好信風，東下三日，便值大風，舶[2]漏水入，商人欲趣小舶[2]，小舶[2]上人，恐人來多，即斫絙斷，商人大怖，命在須臾，恐舶[2]水滿[3]，即取麤財貨，擲著水中，法顯亦以君[4]墀[4]，及澡鑵并餘物，棄擲海中，但恐商人擲去經像，唯一心念觀世音，及歸命漢地衆僧，我遠行求法，願威神歸流，得到所止，如是大風晝夜十三日，到一島邊，潮退之後，見船漏處，即補塞之，於是復前。海中多有抄賊，遇輒無全，大海彌漫無邊，不識東西，唯望日月星宿而進，若陰雨時，爲逐風去，亦無所[5]准，當夜闇時，但見大浪相搏，晃若[6]火色，黿鼉水性，怪[7]異之屬，商人荒懅[8]，不知那向，海深無底，又無下石住處，至天晴已，乃知東西，還復望正而進，若値伏石，則無活路，如是九十許[9]日[9]，乃到一國，名耶婆提，其國外

[1] S, M 止.　[2] S, M 船; and elsewhere.　[3] S, M 漏.　[4] M 軍持.
[5] S, M omit.　[6] S, M 然.　[7] Text has a vulgar form.　[8] S, M 遽.　[9] S, M invert.

當復至西月氏國、若干百年當至于闐國住、若干百年當至屈茨國、若干百年當復來到漢地、[1]若干百年當復至師子國、若干百年當還中天竺、[2]已當上兜術天上、彌勒菩薩見而嘆[3]曰、釋迦文佛鉢至、即共諸天、華香供養七日、七日已、還閻浮提、海龍王將[4]入龍宮。至彌勒將成道時、鉢還分爲四、復本頞[5]那山上、彌勒成道已、四天王當復應念佛、如先佛法、賢劫千佛、共用一[6]鉢。鉢去已、佛法漸滅、佛法滅後、人壽轉短、乃至五歲。五[7]歲之時、粳米酥油、皆悉化滅、人民極惡、捉草[8]木、則變成刀杖、共相傷割殺、其中有福者、逃[9]避入山、惡人相煞盡已、還復來出、共相謂言、昔人壽極長、但爲惡甚、作諸非法、故我等壽命、遂爾短促、乃至五[10]歲、我今共行諸善、起慈悲心、修行信[11]義。如是、各行信義、展轉壽倍、乃至八萬歲。彌勒出世、初轉法輪時、先度釋迦遺法中[12]弟子出家人、及受三歸、五戒、八[13]齋法、供養三寶者、第二、第三次、度有緣者。法顯爾時欲寫此經、其

[1] After 地, S, M insert 住. [2] After 竺, S, M insert 到中天. [3] S, M 歎. [4] S, M 持. [5] S, M 頻. [6] S, M 此. [7] S, M 十. [8] S, M omit. [9] Text, with 外 inside. [10] S, M 十. [11] S, M 仁. [12] S, M omit. [13] S, M omit.

道耶，其便以實答，言是羅漢，既終，王即按經律以羅漢
法葬之，於精舍東四五里，積好大薪，縱廣可三丈餘，高
亦爾，近上著栴檀，沉水，諸香木，四邊作階，上持淨好白
氎，周匝蒙積[1]作[2]大轝，狀[3]似此間轜[4]車，但無龍魚耳，當闍
緒[5]時，王及國人，四衆咸集，以華香供養，從轝至墓所，王
自華香供養，供養訖，轝著積上，酥油遍灌，然後燒之，火
然之時，人人敬心，各脫上服，及羽儀傘蓋，遙擲火中以
助闍維，闍維已，收斂[6]取骨，即以起塔，法顯至不及其生
存，唯見葬時。王篤信佛法，欲爲衆僧作新精舍，先設大
會，飯食僧，供養已，乃選好上牛一雙，金銀寶物，莊校角
上，作好金犂，王自耕[7]墾[8]規[8]郭[8]四邊，然後割給民戶，田宅，
書以鐵券，自是已後，代代相承，無敢廢易。法顯在此國
聞天竺道人，於高座上，誦經云，佛鉢本在毘舍離，今在
揵陀衞，竟若干百年，[9]（法顯聞誦時，有定歲數，但今忘耳）

---

[1] S, M 積. [2] Before 作, S, M insert 上. [3] S, M 牀. [4] S, M 輲. [5] Probably a mistake for 維, as below. [6] S, M 撿. [7] After 耕, S, M insert 頃. [8] S, M omit. [9] The thirteen characters that follow within the parenthetic marks are in all the recensions in two parallel columns in smaller text. They are equivalent to a marginal note with us, and S and M insert a 之 after 誦.

頭布施，投身餧虎，不惜[1]髓腦，如是種種苦行，爲衆生，故成佛，在世四十五年，說法教化，令不安者安，不度者度，衆生緣盡，乃般泥洹，泥洹已來，一千四百九十七歲，[2]世間眼滅，衆生長悲，却後十日，佛齒當出，至[3]無畏山精舍，國內道俗欲殖福者，各各平治道路，嚴飾巷陌，辦衆華香，供養之具，如是唱已，王便[4]夾道兩邊，作菩薩五百身已來，種種變現，或作須大拏，或作睒變，或作象王，或作鹿馬，如是形像，皆彩畫莊校，狀若生人，然後佛齒，乃出中道而行，隨路供養，到無畏精舍，佛堂上，道俗雲集，燒香然燈，種種法事，晝夜不息，滿九十日，乃還城內精舍，城內精舍至齋日，則開門戶禮敬如法。

無畏精舍東四十里，有一山，山中有精舍，名支[5]提，可有二千僧，僧中有一大德沙門，名達摩瞿諦，其國人民，皆共宗仰，住一石室中，四十許年，常行慈心，能感蛇鼠，使同止一室，而不相害。○城南七里，有一精舍，名摩訶毘訶羅，有三千僧住，有一高德沙門，戒行清潔，國人咸疑是羅漢，臨終之時，王來省視，依法集僧而問比丘得

[1] An obsolete form in text. [2] S, M 年. [3] S, M 正. W. [4] S, M 使. [5] S, M 跋.

故以八九圍柱柱樹，樹當柱處心生，遂穿柱而下，入地成根，大可四圍許，柱雖中裂，猶裹其[1]外，人亦不去，樹下起精舍，中有坐像，道俗敬仰無倦。城中又起佛齒精舍，皆七寶作，王淨修梵行，城內人敬[2]信[2]之情亦篤，其國立治已來，無有飢[3]荒喪亂，衆僧庫藏，多有珍寶，無價摩尼，其王入僧庫遊觀，見摩尼珠，卽生貪心，欲奪取之，三日乃悟，卽詣僧中稽首，悔前罪心，因[4]白僧言，願僧立制，自今已後，勿聽王入[5]庫看，比丘滿四十臘，然後得入。其城中多居士長者，薩薄商人，屋宇嚴麗，巷陌平整，四衢道頭皆作說法堂，月八日，十四日，十五日，鋪施高座，道俗四衆皆集聽法。其國人云，都可[6]六萬僧，悉有衆食，王別於城內，供養[7]五六千人，衆食須者，則持大[8]鉢往取，隨器所容，皆滿而還，佛齒常以三月中出之，未出前[9]十日，王莊校大象，使一辯說人，著王衣服，騎象上，擊鼓[10]唱言，菩薩從三阿僧祇劫作[11]行，不惜身命，以國城[12]妻子，及挑眼與人，割肉貿鴿，截

---

[1] Before 其, S has 畏; M 在. [2] S, M invert. [3] M 饑. [4] S, M 告. [5] After 入, S, M insert 其. [6] After 可, M inserts 五. [7] S, M omit. [8] S, M 本. W. [9] S, M omit. [10] Text has 皮 on left. [11] S, M 苦. [12] S, M omit.

皆統屬大洲，多出珍寶珠璣，有出摩尼珠，地方可十里，王使人守護，若有採者十分取三。○其國本無人民，正[1]有鬼神及龍居之，諸國商人共市易，市易時，鬼神不自現身，但出寶物，題其價直，商人則依價，置[2]直取物，因商人來往，故諸國人聞其土樂，悉亦復來，於是遂成大國，其國和適，無冬夏之異，草木常茂，田種隨人，無有時節。佛至其國，欲化惡龍，以神足力，一足躡王城北，一足躡山頂，兩跡相去十五由延，王[3]於[3]城北跡上，起大塔，高四十丈，金銀莊校，衆寶合成，塔邊復起一僧伽藍，名無畏山，有五千僧，起一佛殿，金銀刻鏤，悉以衆寶，中有一青玉像，高二丈許，通身七寶焰光，威相嚴顯，非言所載，右掌中有一無價寶珠，法顯去漢地積年，所與交接，悉異域[4]人，山川草木，舉目無舊，又同行分披[5]，或流[6]或亡，顧影唯已，心常懷悲，忽於此玉像邊，見商人以[7]一白絹扇，供養，不覺悽然，淚下滿目。其國前王，遣使中國，取貝多樹子，於佛殿傍種之，高可二十丈，其樹東南傾，王恐倒，

[1] S, M 止.　[2] S, M 直.　[3] S, M invert.　[4] S, M 城.　[5] M 析.
[6] S, M 留.　[7] After 以, S, M insert 晉地.

此最是廣說備悉者。復得一部抄律，可七千偈，是薩婆多衆律，卽此秦地衆僧所行者也，亦皆師師口相傳授，不書之於文字。復於此衆中得雜阿毘曇心，可六千偈，又得一部[1]經，二千五百偈，又得一卷方等般泥洹經，可五千偈，又得摩訶僧祇阿毘曇，故法顯住此三年，學梵書，梵語，寫律。道整既到中國，見沙門法則，衆僧威儀，觸事可觀，乃追歎秦土邊地，衆僧戒律殘缺，誓言自今已去至得佛，願不生邊地，故遂停不歸。法顯本心欲令戒律流通漢地，於是獨還。○順恒水東下十八由延，其南岸有瞻波大國，佛精舍經行處，及四佛坐處，悉起塔，現有僧住。從此東行，近五十由延，到[2]摩梨帝國，卽是海口，其國有二十四僧伽藍，盡有僧住，佛法亦興，法顯住此二年，寫經及畫像。於是載商人大舶，泛[3]海西南行，得冬初信風，晝夜十四日，到師子國，彼國人云，相去可七百由延。其國本[4]在洲上，東西五十由延，南北三十由延，左右小洲，乃有百數，其間相去，或十里，二十里，或二百里，

---

[1] After 部, S, M insert 綖.　[2] After 到, S, M insert 多.　[3] S 汎.
[4] M 大.

百間，最上有泉水，循石室前，繞房而流，周圍迴曲，如是乃至下重，
順房流，從戶而出，諸僧[1]室中，處處穿石，作窻牖通明，室中朗然，都
無幽闇，其室四角頭穿石作梯蹬上處，今人形小，緣梯上，正得至，
昔人一脚躡處，因名此寺爲波羅越，波羅越者，天竺名鴿也，其寺
中，常有羅漢住。此土丘荒，無人民居，去山極遠，方有村，皆是邪見
不識佛法沙門，婆羅門，及諸異學。彼國人民，常見飛[2]人[2]來入此寺，
于時諸國道人，欲來禮此寺者，彼村人則言，汝何以不飛耶，我見
此間道人皆飛，道人方便答言，翅未成耳。達嚫國幽[3]嶮，道路艱難，
難[4]而知處欲往者，要當賚錢貨施彼國王，王然後遣人送，展轉相
付，示其逕路，法顯竟不得往，承彼土人言，故說之耳。○從波羅奈
國東行，還到巴連弗邑，法顯本求戒律，而北天竺諸國，皆師師口
傳，無本可寫，是以遠步，乃至中天竺，於此摩訶衍僧伽藍，得一部
律，是摩訶僧祇衆律，佛在世時，最初大衆所行也，於祇洹精舍傳
其[5]本，自餘十八部，各有師資，大歸不異，然[6]小小不同，或用開塞，但

[1] S, M 層.　[2] S, M invert.　[3] S, M omit.　[4] S, M omit.　[5] S 具.　[6] S, M 於.

王子，出家學道，却後七日，當成佛，辟支佛聞已，即取泥洹，故名此處爲仙人鹿野苑，世尊成道已，後人於此處起精舍。佛欲度拘驎等五人，五人相謂言，此瞿曇沙門[1]，六年苦行，日食一麻，一米，尚不得道，况入人間，恣身口意，何道之有，今日來者，愼勿與語，佛到，五人皆起作禮處，復北行六十步，佛於此東向坐，始轉法輪，度拘驎等五人處，其北二十步，佛爲彌勒授[2]記處，其南五十步，翳羅鉢龍問佛，我何時[3]得免此龍身，此處皆起塔，見在，中有二僧伽藍，悉有僧住。自鹿野苑精舍，西北行十三由旬[4]，有國名拘睒彌，其精舍名瞿師羅園，佛昔住處，今故有衆僧，多小乘學。從東行八由延，佛本於此度惡鬼處，亦常[5]在此住，經行，坐處，皆起塔，亦有僧伽藍，可百餘僧。○從此南行二百由延，有國名達嚫，是過去迦葉佛僧伽藍，穿[6]大石山作之，凡有五重，最下重，作象形，有五百間石室，第二層作師子形，有四百間，第三層作馬形，有三百間，第四層作牛形，有二百間，第五層作鴿形，有一[7]

[1] After 門, S, M insert 本. [2] S 受. [3] After 時, S, M insert 當.
[4] S, M 延. [5] S, M 嘗. [6] So, S, M. Text has 身 instead of 牙. [7] S, M omit.

常至貝多樹下，悔過自責，受八戒[1]齋，王夫人問，王常遊何處，羣臣答言，恒[2]在貝多樹下，夫人伺王不在時，遣人伐其樹倒，王來見之，迷[3]悶躄地，諸臣以水灑面，良久乃穌，王即以塼累四邊，以百罌牛乳，灌樹根身，四枝[4]布地，作是誓言，若樹不生，我終不起，作[5]是[5]誓已，樹便即根上而生，以至于今[6]，高減十丈。○從此南三里行，到一山名雞足，大迦葉今在此山中，擘[7]山下入，入處不容人，下入極遠有旁孔，迦葉全身在此中住，孔外有迦葉本洗手土，彼方人若頭痛者，以此土[8]塗之，即差。此山中即日故有諸羅漢住，彼彼方諸國道人，年年往供養迦葉，心濃至者，夜即有羅漢來，共言論，釋其疑，已忽然不現。此山榛木茂盛，又多師子，虎狼，不可妄行。○法顯還向巴連弗邑，順恒[2]水西下十由延，得一精舍，名曠野，佛所住處，今現有僧。復順恒[2]水西行十二由延，到迦尸國，波羅柰[9]城，城東北十里許，得仙人鹿野苑精舍，此苑本有辟支佛住，常有野鹿栖宿，世尊將成道，諸天於空中唱言，白淨

[1] S, M omit. [2] Should be 洹. [3] J 迷. R. [4] S, M omit. [5] S, M omit. [6] S, M repeat. [7] S, M 劈. [8] S, M 上. W. [9] Text has 手 on the left.

治罪人，王自念言，鬼王尚能作地獄治罪人，我是人主，何不作地獄治罪人耶，即問臣等，誰能爲我作地獄，主治罪人者，臣答言，唯有極惡人能作耳，王即遣臣，遍求惡人，見池[1]水邊有一人，[2]長壯，黑色，髮黃，目[3]青，以脚鈎魚，[4]口呼[5]禽獸，禽獸來，便射殺無得脫者，得此人已，將來與王，王密勅之，汝作四方高牆，內植種種華果，作好浴池，莊嚴校飾，令人渴仰，牢作門戶，有人入者，輒捉，種種治罪，莫使得出，設使我入，亦治罪莫放，今拜汝作地獄主。[6]時有比丘，次第乞食，入其門，獄卒見之，便欲治罪，比丘惶怖求請，須臾聽我中食。俄頃，復有人入，獄卒內，置碓臼，[7]中擣之，赤沫出，比丘見已，思惟此身無常，苦，空，如泡，如沫，即得阿羅漢，既而獄卒捉內鑊湯中，比丘心顏欣悅，火滅，湯冷，中生蓮華，比丘坐上，爾[8]時，[8]獄卒即往白王，獄中奇怪，願王往看，王言，我前有要，今不敢往，獄卒言，此非小事，王宜疾往，更改先要，王即隨入，比丘爲[9]王說法，王得信解，即壞地獄，悔前所作衆惡，由是信重三寶，

[1] S, M 泄. [2] M omits. [3] S, M 眼. [4] Before 魚, S, M insert 兼. [5] S, M 呼. [6] S, M omit. [7] J 日. [8] S, M omit. [9] S, M omit.

菩薩前到貝多樹下，敷吉祥草，東向而坐，時魔王遣三玉女，從
北來試，魔王自從南來試，菩薩以足指案地，魔兵退散，三女變
成[1]老母[1]，自上苦行六年處，及此諸處，後人皆於中起塔立像，今
皆在。佛成道已，七日觀樹，受解脫樂處，佛於貝多樹下，東西經
行七日處，諸天化作七寶堂[2]，供養佛七日處，文鱗盲龍七日繞
佛處，佛於尼拘律樹下，方石上東向坐，梵天來請佛處，四天王
奉鉢處，五百賈人[3]授麨蜜處，度迦葉兄弟師徒千人處，此諸處，
亦盡[4]起塔。佛得道處，有三僧伽藍，皆有僧住，衆僧民戶，供給繞[5]
足，無所乏少，戒律嚴峻，威儀，坐起，入衆之法，佛在世時，聖衆所
行，以至于今，佛泥洹已來，四大塔處，相承不絶，四大塔者，佛生
處，得道處，轉法輪處，般泥洹處。○阿育王昔作小兒時，當道戲，
遇迦[6]葉[6]佛行乞食，小兒歡喜，即以一掬土施佛，佛持還泥經行
地，因此果報，作鐵輪王，王閻浮提。乘鐵輪，案行閻浮提，見鐵圍
兩山間地獄治罪人，即問羣臣，此是何等，答言，是鬼王閻羅王[7]

---

[1] S, M omit. [2] S, M 臺. [3] S, M 客. [4] S, M omit. [5] S, M 饒. R.
[6] S, M 釋迦. [7] S, M omit.

石，昔有比丘，在上經行，思惟是身無常，苦空，得不淨觀，猒患是身，卽捉刀欲自煞，復念世尊制戒，不得自煞，又念，雖爾，我今但欲煞三毒賊，便以刀自刎，始傷肉，[1]得須陁洹，旣半，得阿那含，斷已，成阿羅漢，果般泥洹。○從此西行四由延，到伽耶城，城內亦空荒。復南行二十里，到菩薩本苦行六年，處處有林木。從此西行三里，到佛入水洗浴，天案樹枝，得攀出池處，又[2]北行二里，得彌家女奉佛乳糜處。從此北行二里，佛於一大樹下，石上東向，坐食糜，樹，石，今悉在，石可廣長六尺，高二尺許，中國寒暑均調，樹木或數千歲，乃至萬歲。從此東北行半由延，到一石窟，菩薩入中西向，結跏趺坐，心念，若我成道，當有神驗，石壁上，卽有佛影現，長三尺許，今猶明亮，時，天地大動，諸天在空中白言，此非[3]是過去當來諸佛成道處，去此西南行，減半由延，[4]到貝多樹下，是過去當來諸佛成道處，諸天說是語已，卽便在前唱導，導引而去，菩薩起行，離樹三十步，天授吉祥草，菩薩受之，復行十五步，五百靑雀飛來，繞菩薩三匝而去，

[1] S, M 再.　[2] M 人.　[3] S, M omit.　[4] S, M omit.

日雖鵰窟山。窟前有四佛坐處，又諸羅漢各各有石窟坐禪處，動
有數百，佛在石室前，東西經行，調達於山北嶮巇[1]間橫擲石，傷佛
足指處，石猶在。佛說法堂已毀壞，止有塼壁基在，其山峰秀端嚴，
是五山中最高。法顯於新城中買香，華，油，燈，倩二舊比丘送，法顯
到[2]耆闍崛山，華香供養，然燈續明，慨然悲傷，收淚而言，佛昔於此[3]
說首楞嚴，法顯生不值佛，但見遺跡處所而已，即於石窟前誦首
楞嚴，停止一宿，還向新城。○出舊城北，行三百餘步，道西，迦蘭陀
竹園精舍今現在，衆僧掃灑。精舍北二三里，有尸磨賒那，尸磨賒
那者，漢言棄死人墓田。搏南山西行，三百步，有一石室，名賓波羅
窟，佛食後，常於此坐禪，又西行五六里，山北陰中，有一石室，名車
帝，佛泥洹後，五百阿羅漢結集經處，出經時，鋪三高[4]座，莊嚴校飾，
舍利弗在左，目連在右，五百數中少一阿羅漢，大迦葉爲上座，時
阿難在門外，不得入，其處起塔，今亦在。搏山亦有諸羅漢坐禪石
窟甚多。出舊城北東，下三里，有調達石室。離此五十步，有大方黑

[1] S 𡾰.　[2] S, M 上.　[3] After 此, S, M insert 住.　[4] S, M 空.

由延，至一小孤石山，山頭有石室，石室南向，佛坐其中，天帝釋將天樂般遮彈琴樂佛處，帝釋以四十二事問佛，一一以指畫石，畫跡故在，此中亦有僧伽藍。從此西南行一由延，到那羅聚落，是舍利弗本生村，舍利弗還於此[1]中般泥洹，即此處起塔，今[2]現在。從此西行一由延，到王舍新城，新城者，是阿闍世王所造，中有二僧伽藍，出城西門三百步，阿闍世王得佛一分舍利，起塔，高大嚴麗。出城南四里，南向入谷，至五山裏，五山周圍，狀若城郭，即是蓱沙王舊城，城東西可五六里，南北七八里，舍利弗，目連，初見頞鞞處，尼揵子作火坑毒飯請佛處，阿闍世王酒飲黑象，欲害佛處，城東北角曲中，耆舊於菴婆羅園中，起精舍，請佛及千二百五十弟子供養處，今故在。其城中空荒，無人住。○入谷搏山，東南上十五里，到耆闍崛山，未至頭三里，有石窟南向，佛本於此坐禪。西北三十步，復有一石窟，阿難於中坐禪，天魔波旬化作雕鷲[3]住窟前，恐阿難，佛以神足力隔石，舒手摩阿難肩，怖即得止，鳥迹手孔今悉在，故

[1] After 此, S, M has 村. [2] After 今, S, M has 亦. [3] Text has the 鳥 beneath.

藍。凡諸中國，唯此國城邑爲大，民人富盛，競行仁義。年年常以建卯月八日行像。作四輪車，縛竹作五層，有羕，櫨[1]榎[1]戟，高二丈餘許，其狀如塔。以白氎纏上，然後彩畫，作諸天形像，以金銀瑠璃莊校其上，懸繒幡蓋，四邊作龕，皆有坐佛，菩薩立侍。可有二十車，車車莊嚴各異。當此日，境內道俗皆集，作倡伎樂，華香供養，婆羅門子來請佛，佛佛次第入城，入城內再宿，通夜然燈，伎樂，供養，國國皆爾。其國長者居士，各於城內，[2]立福德醫藥舍，凡國中貧窮，孤獨，殘跛，一切病人，皆詣此舍，種種供給，醫師看病，隨宜飲食及湯藥，皆令得安，差者自去。阿育王壞七塔，作八萬四千塔，最初所作大塔，在城南三里餘，此塔前有佛[3]迹，起精舍，戶北向，塔[4]南有一石柱，圍丈四五，高三丈餘，上有銘題云，阿育王以閻浮提，布施四方僧，還以錢贖，如是三反。塔北三四百步，阿育王本於此作泥梨城，泥[5]梨[5]城[5]中[6]，有石柱，亦高三丈餘，上有師子，柱上有銘，記作泥梨城因緣，及年數日月。○從此東南行九

[1] M 攎 揠; S 櫨 偃.　[2] S, M 中.　[3] After 佛, S, M insert 脚.
[4] S, M repeat.　[5] S, M omit.　[6] After 中, S, M insert 央.

巴連弗邑是阿育王所治城。城[1]中王宮殿,皆使鬼神作,累石起牆[2]闕,彫文刻鏤,非世所造,今故現在。阿育王弟,得羅漢道,常住耆闍崛山,志樂閑靜,王敬心欲[3]請於家供養,以樂山靜不肯受請,王語弟言,但受我請,當爲汝於城裏作山,乃具飲食,召諸鬼神而告之曰,明日悉受我請,無坐席,各自賚來,明日諸大鬼神,各賚[4]大石來,壁[5]方四五步,坐訖,卽使鬼神累作大石山,又於山底,以五大方石,作一[6]石室,可長三丈,廣二丈,高一丈餘。有一[7]大乘婆羅門子,名羅汰私[8]迷,住此城裏,爽悟多智,事無不達,以清淨自居,國王宗敬師事,若往問訊,不敢竝坐,王設以愛敬心執手,執手已,婆羅門輒自灌洗,年可五十餘,舉國瞻仰,賴此一人,弘宣佛法,外道不能得加陵衆僧。於阿育王塔邊,造摩訶衍僧伽藍,甚嚴麗,亦有小乘寺,都合六七百僧衆,威儀庠序,可觀,四方高德沙門,及學問人,欲求義理,皆詣此寺。婆羅門子師,亦名文殊師利,國內大德沙門,諸大乘比丘,皆宗仰焉,亦住此僧伽

[1] S, M omit. [2] In text with 土 at the side. [3] S, M omit. [4] S, M 持. [5] S, M 辟. [6] S, M omit. [7] S, M omit. [8] After 私, S, M insert 婆.

五百道，俱[1]墮千子口中，賊知是其[2]母，即放弓仗，二父王於是
思惟，皆得辟支佛，二辟支佛塔猶在。後，世尊成道，告諸弟子，
是吾昔時放弓仗處，後人得知，於此處[3]立塔，故以名焉。千小
兒者，即賢劫千佛是也。佛於放弓仗塔邊捨[4]壽，[4]佛[4]告阿難，言，
我却後三月，當般泥洹，魔王嬈固阿難，使不得請佛住世。從
此東行三四里，有塔，佛般泥洹後百年，有毘舍離比丘，錯行
戒律十事，證言佛說如是，爾時諸羅漢及持[5]律比丘，凡[6]有七
百僧，更撿挍律藏，後人於此處起塔，今亦現[7]在。○從此東行
四由延，到五河合口，阿難從摩竭國向毘舍離，欲般泥[8]洹，[8]諸
天告阿闍世王，阿[9]闍[9]世[9]王[9]即自嚴駕，將士衆追到河上，毘舍
離諸梨車聞阿難來，亦復來迎，俱到河上，阿難思惟，前，則阿
闍世王致恨，還，則梨車復怨，即[10]於河中央入火光三昧，燒身
而般泥洹，分身作二分，一分在一岸邊，於是二王各得半身
舍利，還歸起塔。○度河南下一由延，到摩竭提國，巴連弗邑，

[1] S, M omit. [2] S, M 我. [3] S, M omit. [4] S, M omit. [5] After 持, S, M insert 戒. [6] After 凡, S, M insert 夫者. [7] S, M omit. [8] S, M 涅槃. [9] S, M omit. [10] S, M 則.

作信，遣還其家處[1]，立石柱，上有銘題。○自此東行十[2]由延，到毘舍離國。毘舍離城北大林，重閣精舍，佛住處，及阿難半身塔。其城裏本菴婆羅女家，爲佛起塔，今故現在。城南三里，道西，菴婆羅女以園施佛作佛住處。佛將般泥洹，與諸弟子出毘舍離城，西門，廻身右轉顧看毘舍離城，告諸弟子，是吾最後所行處，後人於此處起塔。城西北三里，有塔名放弓仗，以名此者，恒水流有一國王，王小夫人，生一肉胎，大夫人妒之，言，汝生不祥之徵，即盛以木函，擲恒水中，下流有國王遊觀，見水上木函，開看，見千小兒，端正殊特，王即取養之，遂便長大，甚勇健，所往征伐，無不摧伏，次伐父王本國，王大愁憂，小夫人問[3]如何故愁憂，王曰，彼國王有千子，勇健無比，欲求[4]伐吾國，是以愁耳，小夫人言，王勿愁憂，但於城東作高樓，賊來時，置我樓上，則我能却之，王如其言，至賊來[5]時，小夫人於樓上，語賊言，汝是我子，何故作反逆事，賊曰，汝是何人云是我母，小夫人曰，汝等若不信者，盡仰向張口，小夫人即以兩手[6]搆兩乳，乳作[7]

---

[1] S, M omit. [2] S, M 五. [3] S, M 王. [4] J 來. [5] S, M 到. [6] S, M 于. W.
[7] Before 作, S, M insert 各.

法顯傳

已，語王言，汝供養[1]若能勝是，便可壞之持去，吾不與汝諍，阿育王知其供養具，非世之所[2]有，於是便還。此中荒蕪，無人灑掃，常有羣象，以鼻取水灑地，取雜華香而供養。諸國有道人來，欲禮拜塔，遇象大怖，依樹自翳，見象如法供養，道人大自悲感，此中无有僧伽藍，可供養此塔，乃令象灑掃，道人即捨大戒，還作沙彌，自挽草木，平治處所，使得淨潔，勸化國王作僧住處，已爲寺主[3]，今現有僧住，此事在近，自爾相承至今，恒[4]以沙彌爲寺主。

○從此東行三由延，大[5]子遣車匿白馬還處，亦起塔。從此東行四由延，到炭塔，亦有僧伽藍。復東行十二由延，到拘夷那竭城，城北，雙樹間，希連禪[6]河邊，世尊於此北首而般泥洹，及須跋最後得道處，以金棺供養世尊七日處，金剛力士放金杵處，八王分舍利處，諸處皆起塔，有僧伽藍，今悉現在。其城中人民亦希[7]曠，止有衆僧民戶。從此東南行十二由延，到諸梨車欲逐[8]佛般泥洹處，而佛不聽，戀佛不肯去，佛化作大深塹[9]，不得渡，佛與鉢

---

[1] S, M omit. [2] S, M omit. [3] S, M omit. [4] So, but should be 恆. [5] J 太. R.
[6] S, M omit. [7] S, M 稀. [8] S 遂. [9] In text, with 水 at the side.

佛得道，還見父王處，五百釋子出家，向優波離作禮，地六種震動處，佛爲諸天說法，四天王等[1]守四門，父王不得入處，佛在尼拘律樹下東向坐，大愛道布施佛僧伽梨處，此樹猶在。瑠[2]璃王煞[3]釋種，[4]釋種[4]死，[5]盡得須陀洹，立塔，今亦在。城東北數里，有王田，太子坐[6]樹下，觀耕者處。城東五十里，有王園，園名論民，夫人入池洗浴，出池北岸二十步，舉手攀樹枝，東向生太子，太子墮地，行七步，二龍王浴太子身，浴處遂作井，及上洗浴池，今衆僧常取飲之。凡諸佛有四處常定，一者，成道處，二者，輪[7]法輪處，三者，說法，論議伏外道處，四者，上忉利天，爲母說法來下處，餘者[8]則隨時示現焉。迦維羅衞國大空荒，人民希疎，道路怖畏白象，師子，不可妄行。○從佛生處東行五由延，有國名藍莫，此國王得佛一分舍利，還歸起塔，即名藍莫塔，塔邊有池，池中有龍，常守護此塔，晝夜供養，阿育王出世，欲破八塔，作八萬四千塔，破七塔已，次欲破此塔，龍便現身，持阿育王入其宮中，觀諸供養具，

[1] S, M omit. [2] S 琉. [3] S, M 殺. [4] After 種, S, M insert 子. [5] S, M 先. [6] S, M omit. [7] Probably should be 轉. [8] S, M omit.

世[1]，各有徒衆，亦皆乞食，但不持鉢，亦復求福，於曠路側，立福德舍屋宇，牀臥，飲食，供給行路人，及出家人，來去客，但所期異耳。調達亦有衆在，常[2]供養過去三佛，唯不供養釋迦文佛。舍衞城東南四里，琉璃王欲伐舍夷國，世尊當道側立，立處起塔。○城西五十里，到一邑，名都維，是迦葉佛本生處，父子相見處，般泥洹處，皆悉起塔，迦葉如來全身舍利亦起大塔。從舍衞城東南，行十二由延，到一邑，名那毘伽，是拘樓秦佛所生處，父子相見處，般泥洹處，亦[3]皆[4]起塔。從此北行，減一由延，到一邑，是拘那含牟尼佛所生處，父子相見處，般泥洹處，亦皆起塔。○從此東行，減一由延，到迦維羅衞城，城中都無王民，甚[5]丘[6]荒，止[7]有衆僧民戶，數十家而已。白淨王故宮處，作太子母形像，及[8]太子乘白馬[9]入母胎時，太子出城東門見病人，廻車還處，皆起塔。阿夷相太子處，與難陀等撲象，捔射處，箭東南去三十里入地，令[10]泉水出，後世人治作井，令行人飲[11]，

[1] S, M omit. [2] S, M omit. [3] After 亦, S, M insert 有僧伽藍.
[4] S, M omit. [5] After 甚, S, M insert 如. [6] S, M 坵. [7] S, M 只.
[8] S, M 乃. W. [9] ? Mistake for 象. [10] S 今. [11] After 飲, S, M insert 之.

居士，人民，皆雲集而聽，時外道女，名旃遮[1]摩那起嫉妬[2]心，及[3]懷衣著，腹前，似若妊[4]身，於衆會中謗佛以非法，於是天帝釋即化作白鼠，嚙[5]其腰帶[6]，帶斷，所懷衣墮地，地即[7]裂，生入地獄，及調達毒爪[8]欲害佛，生入地獄處，後人皆標[9]幟[9]之，又於論議處起精[10]舍[10]，高六丈許，中[11]有坐佛像[12]，其道東有外道天寺，名曰影覆，與論議處精舍挾[13]道相對，亦高六丈許，所以名影覆者，日在西時，世尊精舍影則映外道天寺，日在東時，外道天寺影則北映，終不得映佛精舍也，外道常遣人守其天寺，掃灑，燒香，燃燈，供養，至明旦其燈輒移在佛精舍中，婆羅門恚言，諸沙門取我燈，自供養佛，爲爾[14]不止。婆羅門於是夜自伺候，見其所事天神，將[15]燈繞佛精舍三匝[16]，供[17]養[17]，供養佛已，忽然不見，婆羅門乃知佛神大，即捨家入道，傳云，近有此事。繞祇洹精舍有九十八僧伽藍，盡有僧住[18]，唯一處空。此中國有九十六種外道，皆知今世後[19]

---

1 S, p.y. 栴.　2 S, M 妒.　3 Should probably be 乃.　4 S, M 娠.
5 S, M 齧.　6 S, M omit.　7 After 即, S, M insert 劈.　8 J 瓜.
9 S, M 標識.　10 S, M repeat.　11 S, M 裏.　12 S, M omit.　13 S, M 夾.
14 Another form of this in text.　15 S, M 持.　16 S, M 帀.　17 S, M omit.
18 After 住, S, M insert 處.　19 S, M omit.

作兩重，還移像本處。法顯、道整，初到祇洹精舍，念昔世尊住此二十五年，自傷生在邊地，[1] 共諸同志遊歷諸國，而或有還者，或有無常者，今日乃見佛空處，愴然心悲。彼衆僧出問法[2] 顯等言，汝從何國來，答曰，[3] 從漢地來。彼衆僧歎曰，奇哉，邊國[4] 之人，乃能求法至此，自相謂言，我等諸師和上，[5] 相承以[6] 來，未見漢道人來到此也。精舍西北四里，有林，[7] 名曰得眼，本有五百盲人，依精舍住此，佛為說法，盡還得眼，盲人歡喜，刺[8] 杖著地，頭面作禮，杖遂生長大，世人重之，無敢伐者，遂成為林，[7] 是故以得眼為名。祇洹衆僧，中食後，多往彼林[7] 中坐禪。祇洹精舍東北六七里，毘舍佉母作精舍，請佛及僧，此處故在。祇洹精舍大院，[9] [10] 各有二門，一門東向，一門北向，此園即須達長者布金錢買地處，[11] 精舍當中央，佛住此處最久，說法，度人，經行，坐處，亦盡起塔，皆有名字，乃孫陀利殺身謗佛處。出祇洹東門，北行七十步，道西，佛昔共九十六種外道論議，國王，大臣，

[1] S, M 夷.　[2] S, M omit.　[3] S, M 云.　[4] S, M 地.　[5] M 尚.
[6] S, M 已.　[7] S, M 榛.　[8] S, M. The Corean text is a vulgar form of this.
[9] S 援; M 園.　[10] S, M 落.　[11] After 處, S, M insert 也.

波斯匿王所治城也。大愛道故精舍處，須達長者井壁，及鴦掘魔得道，般泥洹燒身處，後人起塔，皆在此城中，諸外道婆羅門，生嫉妬心，欲毀壞之，天即雷電霹靂，終不能得壞。出城南門，千二百步，道西，長者須達起精舍，精舍東向，開門[1]戶，兩邊[2]有二石柱，左柱上作輪形，右柱上作牛形，精[3]舍[3]左[3]右，[3]池流清淨，樹[4]林[5]尚茂，衆華異色，蔚然可觀，即所謂祇洹精舍也，佛上忉利天，爲母說法九十日，波斯匿王思見佛，即刻牛頭栴檀作佛像，置佛坐處，佛後還入精舍，像即避出迎佛，佛言，還坐，吾般泥洹後，可爲四部衆作法式，像即還坐，此像最是衆像之始，後人所法者也，佛於是移住南邊小精舍，與像異處，相去二十步。祇洹精舍，本有七層，諸國王人民，競興供養，懸繒幡[6]蓋，散華燒香，然[7]燈續明，日日不絕，鼠含[8]燈炷，燒[9]幡[6]蓋，遂及精舍，七重都盡，諸國王人民，皆大悲惱，謂栴檀像已燒，却後四五日，開東小精舍戶，忽見本像，皆大歡喜，共治精舍，得

---

[1] J repeats. [2] S, M 廊. [3] S, M omit. [4] S, M omit. [5] After 林, S, M insert 木. [6] S, M 旛. [7] S, M 燃. [8] S, M 銜. [9] After 燒, S, M insert 花.

見國王言，汝能如是者，我當多將兵衆住此，益積糞穢，汝復能除不，鬼神即起大風，吹之令淨。此處有百枚小塔，人終日數之，不能得知，若至意欲知者，便一塔邊置一人，已復計數人人，或多或少，其不可得知。有一僧伽藍，可六七百僧，此中有辟支佛食處，泥[1]地大如車輪，餘處生草，此處獨不生，及曬衣地處，亦不生草，衣條[2]著地跡，今故現在。○法顯住龍精舍，夏坐，坐訖，東南行七由延，到罽饒[3]夷城，城接恒[4]水，有二僧伽藍，盡小乘學。去城西六七里，恒[4]水北岸，佛爲諸弟子說法處，傳云，說無常，苦，空[5]，說身如泡沫等，此處起塔，猶在。度恒[4]水，南行三由延，到一村[6]，名阿梨，佛於此中說法，經行，坐處，盡起塔。○從此東南行十由延，到沙祇大國，出沙祇城，南門道東，佛本在此嚼楊枝，已[7]，刺土中，即生長七尺，不增不減，諸外道婆羅門嫉妬，或斫或拔，遠棄之，其處續生如故。此中亦有四佛經行，坐處，起塔，故在。○從此南行八由延，到拘薩羅國舍衞城，城內人民希曠，都有二百餘家，即

[1] After 泥, S, M insert 洹. [2] S, M 條. [3] S, p.y. 鐃. [4] So, all recensions and Julien. Probably should always be 洹. [5] S, M omit. [6] S, M 林. [7] S, M omit.

退。佛以受天食三月，故身作天香，不同世人，即便浴身，後人於
此處起浴室，浴室猶在。優鉢羅比丘尼初禮佛處，今亦起塔，佛
在世時，有剪[1]髮爪[2]，作塔，及過去三佛，并釋迦文佛坐處，經行處，
及作諸佛形像處，盡有塔，今悉在。天帝釋，梵天王，從佛下處，亦
起塔。此處僧及尼可有千人，皆同衆食，雜大小乘學，住處有[3]一
白耳龍，與此衆僧作檀越，令國內豐熟，雨澤以時，無諸災害，使
衆僧得安，衆僧感其惠，故爲作龍舍，敷置坐處，又爲龍設福食
供養，衆僧日日衆中，別差三人，到龍舍中食，每至夏坐訖，龍輒
化形，作一小蛇，兩耳邊白，衆僧識之，銅盂盛酪，以龍置中，從上
座至下座行之，似若問訊，遍便化去，每[4]年一出，其國豐饒，人民
熾盛，最樂無比，諸國人來，無不經理供給所須。寺西[5]北五十由
延，有一寺名大[6]墳[6]，大墳者，惡鬼名也，佛本化是惡鬼，後人於此
處起精舍布[7]施阿羅漢，以水灌手，水瀝滴地，其處故在，正復掃
除，常現不滅。此處別有佛塔，善鬼神常掃灑，初不須人工，有邪

[1] S, M 翦. [2] S, M 爪. W. [3] S, M omit. [4] S, M 年. [5] S, M omit.
[6] S, M 火境. [7] After 舍, S, M insert 以精舍.

以天眼遙見世尊，卽語尊者大目連，汝可往問訊世尊，目連卽往，頭面禮足，共相問訊，問訊已，佛語目連，吾却後七日，當下閻浮提，目連既還，于時八國大王，及諸臣民，不見佛久，咸皆渴仰，雲集此國，以待世尊，時優鉢羅比丘尼，卽自心念，今日國王臣民，皆當[1]迎佛，我是女人，何由得先見，佛卽以神足化作轉輪聖王，最前禮佛。佛從忉利天上來向下，下時，化作三道寶階，佛在中道，七寶階上行，梵天王，亦化作白銀階，在右邊執白拂而侍，天帝釋化作紫金階，在左邊執七寶蓋而侍，諸天無數從佛下，佛既下，三階俱沒于[2]地，餘有七級而[3]現，後阿育王，欲知其根際，遣人掘看，下至黃泉，根猶不盡，王益敬[4]信[4]，卽於階上起精舍，當中階作丈六立像，精舍後立石柱，高三十肘，上作師子，柱內四邊，有佛像，內外暎[5]徹，淨若瑠璃，有外道論師，與沙門諍此住處，時沙門理屈，於是共立誓言，此處若是沙門住處者，今當有靈驗，作是言已，柱頭師子，乃大鳴吼見驗[6]，於是外道慴[7]怖，心伏而

[1] After 當, S, M insert 奉. R. [2] S, M 於. [3] S, M omit. [4] S, M invert. [5] S, M 映. [6] S, M 證. [7] S, M 懼.

已，復問其臘數，次第得房舍臥具，種種如法。衆僧住處，作舍利弗塔，目連，阿難塔，幷阿毘曇，律，經塔。安居後一月，諸希福之家，勸化供養僧，行[1]非時漿，衆僧大會說法，說法已，供養舍利弗塔，種種華[2]香[2]，通夜然燈，使伎[3]樂[3]人[4]作，舍利弗，大[5]婆羅門時，詣佛求出家，大目連，大迦葉，亦如是，諸比丘尼，多供養阿難塔，以阿難請世尊聽女人出家故。諸沙彌，多供養羅云。阿毘曇師者，供養阿毘曇，律師者供養律，年年一供養，各自有日，摩訶衍人，則供養般若波羅蜜，文殊師利，觀世音等。衆僧受歲竟，長者居士，婆羅門等，各將[6]種種衣物，沙門所須以用[7]，布施衆[8]僧[8]，僧受[9]，亦自各各布施，佛泥洹已來，聖衆所行，威儀法則，相承不絕。自度[10]新頭河，至南天竺，迄于南海，四五萬里，皆平坦，無大山川，正有河水耳[11]。○從此東南行十八由延，有國名僧伽施，佛上忉利天，三月爲母說法，來[12]下處。佛上忉利天，以神通力，都不使諸弟子知，來滿七日，乃放神足，阿那律

[1] S, M 作.　[2] S, M invert.　[3] S, M omit.　[4] Before 人, S, M have 彼.　[5] S, M 本.　[6] S, M 持.　[7] S, M omit.　[8] S, M invert.　[9] S, M omit.　[10] S, M 渡　[11] S, M omit.　[12] S, M 未. R.

則脫天冠，共諸宗親羣臣，手自行食，行食已，鋪氈於地，對上座前，坐於衆僧前，不敢坐牀，佛在世時，諸王供養法式，相傳至今。從是以南，名爲中國，中國，寒暑調和，無霜雪，人民殷樂，無戶籍官法，唯耕王地者，乃輸地利，欲去便去，欲住便住，王治不用刑斬[1]有罪者，但罰其錢，隨事輕重，雖復謀爲惡逆，不過截右手而已，王之侍衞左右，皆有供祿，舉國人民，悉不殺生，不飲酒，不食葱蒜，唯除旃荼[2]羅，旃荼羅名爲惡人，與人別居，若入城市，則擊木[3]以自異，人則識而避之，不相搪[4]揬[5]。國中不養豬[6]雞[6]，不賣生口，市無屠店[7]，及沽[8]酒者，貨易，則用貝齒，唯旃荼羅，漁[9]獵師，賣肉耳。自佛般泥洹後，諸國王，長者居士，爲衆僧起精舍，供給田宅園圃，民戶，牛犢，鐵券書錄，後王王相傳，無敢廢者，至今不絕。衆僧住止房舍[10]，牀蓐飲食，衣服，都無闕乏，處處皆爾。衆僧常以作功德爲業，及誦經坐禪，客僧往到，舊僧迎逆，代擔[11]衣鉢，給洗足水，塗足油，與非時漿，須臾息

[1] S, M 罰. [2] S, M 茶. W. [3] S 水. [4] S 唐; S, p.y. 湯. [5] S 突. [6] S, M 猪 雞. [7] S, M 估. [8] S 估; M 酤. [9] S, M omit. [10] After 舍, S, M insert 供養. [11] S, M 檐. W.

能及。彼國人傳云，千佛盡當於此留影。影西四[1]百步許，佛在時，剃髮剪爪，佛自與諸弟子，共造塔，高七八丈，以爲將來塔法，今猶在，邊有寺，寺中有七百餘僧。此處有諸羅漢，辟支佛塔，乃千數。○住此冬三月，法顯等三人，南度小雪山，雪山冬夏積雪，山北陰中，遇[2]寒風暴起，人皆噤戰，慧景一人，不堪復進，口出白沫，語法顯云，我亦不復活，便可時去，勿得俱死，於是遂終，法顯撫之，悲號本圖不果，命也奈何。復自力前，得過嶺南，到羅夷國，近有三千僧，兼大小乘學。住此夏坐，坐訖，南下行十日，到跋那國，亦有三千許僧，皆小乘學。從此東行三日，復渡新頭河，兩岸皆平地。○過河有國名毘荼，佛法興盛，兼大小乘學，見秦道人往，乃大憐愍，作是言，如何邊地人能知出家爲道，遠求佛法，悉供給所須，待之如法。○從此東南行，減八十由延，經歷諸寺甚多，僧衆萬數，過是諸處已，到一國，國名摩頭羅，又經蒱[3]那河，河邊左右，有二十僧伽藍，可有三千僧，佛法轉盛。凡沙河已西，天竺諸國，國王皆篤信佛法，供養衆僧時，

[1] S, M omit.　[2] S, J 過.　[3] S, M 捕.

後、精舍人、則登高樓、擊大鼓、吹蠡[1]、戢銅鉢[2]、王聞已、則詣精舍、以華香供養、供養已、次第頂戴而去、從東門入、西門出、王朝朝如是供養禮拜、然後聽國政、居士長者亦先供養、乃修家事、日日如是、初無懈[3]倦。供養都訖、乃還頂骨於精舍中、有七寶解脫塔、或開或閉、高五尺許、以盛之。精舍門前、朝朝恒有賣華香人、凡欲供養者、種種買焉、諸國王亦恒遣使供養。精舍處方三[4]十步、雖復天震地裂、此處不動。從此北行一由延、到那竭國城、是菩薩本以銀錢貿五莖華、供養定光佛處。城中亦有佛齒塔、供養如頂骨法。城東北一由延、到一谷口、有佛錫杖、亦起精舍供養、杖以牛頭栴檀作、長丈六七許、以木筒盛之、正復百千人舉、不能移。入谷口[5]西行、有佛僧伽梨、亦[6]起[7]精舍供養、彼國土俗[8]亢旱時、國人相率出衣、禮拜供養、天即大雨。那竭城南半由延、有石室博山西南向、佛留影此中、去十餘步觀之、如佛真形、金色相好、光明炳著、轉近轉微、髣髴如有、諸方國王遣工畫師摹寫、莫

[1] S, M 螺.　[2] S, M 鈸.　[3] The Corean text has the 心 beneath.
[4] S, M 四.　[5] After 口, S, M insert 四日.　[6][7] S, M omit.　[8] S, M omit.

伏地，不能得前，更作四輪車載鉢，八象共牽，復不能進，王知與鉢緣未至，深自愧歎，卽於此處起塔及僧伽藍，幷留鎭守，種種供養。可有七百[1]餘僧，日將欲[2]中，衆僧則出鉢，與白衣等，種種供養，然後中食，至暮燒香時，復爾，可容二斗許，雜色而黑多，四際分明，厚可二分，甚[3]光澤，貧人以少華投中，便滿，有大富者，欲以多華[4]供養，正復百千萬斛，終不能滿。寶雲僧景，止[5]供養佛鉢，便還。慧景，慧達，道整，先向那竭國，供養佛影，佛齒，及頂骨，慧景病，道整住看，慧達一人，還於弗樓沙國相見，而慧達，寶雲，僧景，遂還秦土。慧景[6]在佛鉢寺無常，由是法顯獨進向佛頂骨所。

○西行十六由延，至那竭國界，醯[7]羅城，城[8]中有佛頂骨精舍，盡以金薄七寶校飾，國王敬重頂骨，慮人抄奪，乃取國中豪姓八人，人持一印，印封守護，淸晨八人俱到，各視其印，然後開戶，開戶已，以香汁洗手，出佛頂骨，置精舍外，高座上，以七寶圓碪，碪下，瑠璃鍾覆上，皆珠璣校飾，骨黃白色，方圓四寸，其上隆起，每日出

[1] S, M 日. W. [2] S, M omit. [3] S, M omit, and insert 瑩徹. [4] After 華, S, M insert 而. [5] S, M 只. [6] After 景, S, M insert 應. [7] S, M 醯. [8] S, M omit.

阿育王子，法益，所治處，佛爲菩薩時，亦於此國以眼施人，其處亦起大塔，金銀校餝。此國人，多小乘學。〇自此東行七日，有國名竺刹尸羅，竺刹尸羅，漢言截頭也，佛爲菩薩時，於此處以頭施人，故因以爲名。復東行二日，至投身餧餓虎處，此二處亦起大塔，皆衆寶校飾，諸國王，臣民，競興供養，散華然燈，相繼不絶，通上二塔，彼方人亦名爲四大塔也。〇從犍陁衞國，南行四日，到弗樓沙國，佛昔將諸弟子，遊行此國，語阿難云，吾般泥洹後，當有國王，名罽膩伽，於此處起塔。後罽[1]膩伽王出世，出行遊觀時，天帝釋欲開發其意，化作牧牛小兒，當道起塔，王問言[2]，汝作何等，答言作佛塔，王言大善，於是王即於小兒塔上起塔，高四十餘丈，衆寶校飾，凡所經見塔廟，壯麗威嚴，都無此比，傳云，閻浮提塔，唯此塔[3]爲上，王作塔成已，小塔即自傍出大塔南，高三尺許。佛鉢即在此國，昔月氏王，大興兵衆，來伐此國，欲取佛鉢，既伏此國已，月氏王等[4]，篤信佛法，欲持鉢去，故大[5]興供養，供養三寶畢，乃校飾大象，置鉢其上，象便

[1] S, M omit.　[2] S, M 曰.　[3] S, M omit.　[4] S, M omit.　[5] S, M omit.

者，像立在佛泥洹後三百許年許[1]於周氏平王時，由茲而言，大教宣流，始自此像，非夫彌勒大士繼軌釋迦，孰能令三寶宣通，邊人識法，固知冥運之開，本非人事，則漢明帝[2]之夢有由而然矣。○度河便到烏長國，其[3]烏長[4]國是正北天竺也，盡作中天竺語，中天竺所謂中國，俗人衣服飲食，亦與中國同，佛法甚盛，名衆僧止[5]住[5]處爲僧伽藍，凡有五百僧伽藍，皆小乘學，若有客比丘到，悉供養三日，三日過已，乃令自求所安。常傳言，佛至北天竺，卽到此國也，[6]佛遺足跡於此，[7]或長或短，在人心念，至今猶爾，及曬衣石，度惡龍處，悉[8]亦[8]現在，石高丈四尺，[9]闊二丈許，一邊平。慧景，慧[10]達，[10]道[11]整[11]三人，先發向佛影那竭國，法顯等住此國，夏坐。坐訖，南下到宿呵多國。○其國佛法亦盛。昔天帝釋試菩薩，化作鷹鴿，割肉貿鴿處，佛旣[12]成道，與諸弟子遊行，語云，此本是吾割肉貿鴿處，國人由是得知，於此處起塔，金銀校飾。○從此東下五日，行到犍陀[13]衞國，是

---

1 Probably for 計, a cutter's mistake. 2 S, M omit. 3 S, M omit. 4 S, M 萇. 5 S, M invert. 6 S, M 已. 7 After 此, S, M insert 跡. 8 S, M invert. 9 S, M omit. 10 11 S, M invert. 12 S, M 卽. 13 S, M 陁.

褐爲異沙門法用轉[1]勝，不可具記。其國當葱嶺之中，自葱嶺已前，草木果實皆異，唯竹及安石榴[2]甘蔗三物，與漢地同耳。

〇從此西行，向北天竺，在道一月，得度葱嶺，葱嶺山[3]冬夏有[4]雪，又有毒龍，若失其意，則吐毒風，雨雪，飛沙，礫石，遇此難者，萬無一全，彼土人[5]即名爲雪山[6]也。度嶺已，到北天竺，始入其境，有一小國，名陀歷，亦有衆僧，皆小乘學。其國昔有羅漢，以神足力，將一巧匠上兜率[7]天，觀彌勒菩薩長短，色貌，還下刻木作像，前後三上觀，然後乃成像，長八丈，足趺八尺，齋日常有光明，諸國王競與供養，今故現在。〇於此順嶺，西南行十五日，其道艱岨，崖岸嶮絕，其山唯石壁立千仞，臨之目眩，欲進則投足無所，下有水，名新頭河，昔人有鑿石通路，施傍梯者，凡度七百，度梯已，躡懸絙過河，河兩岸相去，減八十步，九譯[8]所記，漢之張騫，甘英，皆不至此[9]。衆僧問法顯佛法東過，其始可知耶，顯云，訪問彼土人，皆云古老相傳，自立彌勒菩薩像後，便有天竺沙門，賫經律過此河

---

[1] S, M repeat. [2] S, M 留. [3] S, M omit. [4] J 日. [5] S, M repeat.
[6] After 山, S, M insert 人. [7] S, M 術. [8] S, M 驛. [9] S, M omit.

國，在道二十五日，便到其國。國王精進，有千餘僧，多大乘學。住此十五日已，於是南行四日，入葱嶺山，到於麾國安居。安居已，山[1]行二十五日，到竭叉國，與慧景等合。○值其國王作般遮越師。般遮越師，漢言五年大會也。會時，請四方沙門，皆來雲集[2]。已，莊嚴衆僧坐處，懸繒幡[3]蓋，作金銀蓮華，著僧[4]座後，鋪淨坐具，王及羣臣，如法供養，或一月二月，或三月，多在春時。王作會已，復勸諸羣臣，設供供養，或一日，二日，三日，五日，乃[5]至[5]七[5]日[5]。供養都畢，王以所乘馬，鞍勒自副，使國中貴重臣騎之，并諸白[6]㲲[6]種種珍寶，沙門所須之物，共諸羣臣發願布施衆[7]僧[7]。布施僧[8]已，還從僧贖。其地山寒，不生餘穀，唯熟麥[9]耳。衆僧受歲已，其晨輒霜，故其王每請[10]衆僧令麥熟，然後受歲。其國中有佛唾壺，以石作之，[11]色似佛鉢，又有佛一齒，其[12]國中[13]人，爲佛齒起塔，有千餘僧徒，[14]盡小乘學。自山以東，俗人被服粗，[15]類[15]與[15]秦土同，[16]亦以氈

[1] S, M 止.　[2] J repeats.　[3] S, M 旛.　[4] S, M 繒.　[5] S, M omit.
[6] S, p. y. 自㲲.　[7] S, M omit.　[8] S, M omit.　[9] S, M 麥.　[10] S, M 讃.
[11] S, M omit.　[12] S, M omit.　[13] S, M omit.　[14] S, M omit.　[15] S, M omit.
[16] S, M omit.

行像，停三月日。其國中有[1]四大僧伽藍，不數小者，從四月一日，城裏便掃灑道路，莊嚴巷陌，其城門上張大幃幕，事事嚴飾，[2]王及夫人婇[3]女，皆住其中。瞿摩帝僧是大乘學，王所敬重，最先行像，離城三四里，作四輪像車，高三丈餘，狀如行殿，七寶莊校，懸繒幡蓋，像立車中，二菩薩侍，作諸天侍從，皆以[4]金銀彫瑩，懸於虛空。像去門百步，王脫天冠，易著新衣，徒跣持華香，翼從出城迎像，頭面禮足，散花[5]燒香，像入城時，門樓上夫人婇[3]女，遙散衆花，[5]紛紛而下。如是莊嚴供具，車車各異，一僧伽藍則一日行像，[6]自月一日爲始，至十四日行像乃訖。行像訖，王及夫人乃還宮耳。其城西七八里，有僧伽藍，名王新寺，作來八十年，經三王方成，可高二十五丈，彫文刻鏤，金銀覆上，衆寶合成，塔後作佛堂，莊嚴妙好，梁柱，戶扇，牕[7]牖，皆以金薄，別作僧房，亦嚴麗整飾，非言可盡，嶺東六國諸王所有上價寶物，多作供養，人用者少。○

既過四月行像，僧韶一人，隨胡道人向罽賓。法顯等進向子合

---

[1] S, M 十.　[2] S, M 餝.　[3] S, M 采.　[4] S, M omit.　[5] S, M 華.
[6] S, M 四.　[7] S 窻; M 窓.

小乘學，諸國俗人及沙門，盡行天竺法，但有精麤[1]。從此西行，所經諸國，類皆如是。唯國國胡語不同，然出家人皆習天竺書、天竺語。住此一月日，復西北行十五日，到烏[2]夷國。[3]僧亦有四千餘人，皆小乘學。法則齊整，秦土沙門至彼，都不豫其僧例也[4]。法顯得符行當[5]公孫經理，住二月餘日，於是還與寶雲等共合[6]。烏夷國人不修禮義，遇客甚薄，智嚴、慧簡、慧嵬遂返向高昌，欲求行資。法顯等蒙符公孫供給，遂得直進西南行，路中無居民，涉行艱難，所經之苦，人理莫比。在道一月五日，得到于闐。○其國豐樂，人民殷盛，盡皆奉法，以法樂相娛。衆僧乃數萬人，多大乘學，皆有衆食。彼國人民星居，家家門前皆起小塔，最小者可高二丈許。作四方僧房，供給客僧及餘所須。國主安頓[7]供[8]給[8]法顯等於僧伽藍。僧伽藍名瞿摩帝，是大乘寺，三千僧共犍槌[9]食。入食堂時，威儀齊肅，次第而坐，一切寂然，器鉢無聲，淨人益食，不得相喚，但以手指麾。慧景、道整、慧達先發向竭叉國，法顯等欲觀

[1] S 麄. [2] S, M 僞. [3] After 國, S, M repeat 僞夷國. [4] S, M omit. [5] S, M 堂. [6] S, M 爲. [7] S, M 堵. [8] S, M omit. [9] S, M 椎.

高僧法顯傳[1]

東晉沙門釋法顯自記遊天竺事[2]

法顯昔在長安，慨律藏殘缺，於是遂以弘始二年，歲在己亥，與慧景，道整，慧應，慧嵬等，同契至天竺，尋求戒律。初發跡長安，度隴，至乾歸國，夏坐。夏坐訖，前[3]至耨[4]檀國，度養樓山，至張掖鎮，張掖大亂，道路不通。張掖王慇懃，遂留爲作檀越。於是與智嚴，慧簡，僧紹，寶雲，僧景等相遇，欣於同志，便共夏坐。夏坐訖，復進到燉煌，有塞東西可八十里，南北四十里，共停一月餘日，法顯等五人隨使先發，復與寶雲等別。燉煌太守李浩供給度沙河。沙河中，多有惡鬼熱風，遇則皆死，無一全者。上無飛鳥，下無走獸，遍望極目，欲求度處，則莫知所擬，唯以死人枯骨爲標幟耳。〇行十七日，計可千五百里，得至鄯[5]鄯[5]國，其地崎嶇薄瘠，俗人衣服粗，與漢地同，但以氈褐爲異。其國王奉法，可有四千餘僧，悉

[1] S, M omit. [2] S, M omit. [3] After 前, S, M insert 行. [4] S, M 褥. [5] M 善.

高麗國大藏都監雕造

日本
安永己亥沙門玄韻重鐫

沙門法顯自記遊天竺事

西曆一千八百八十五年
英國牛津大學校印書局刊著